TRUE GHOST STORIES

New York

Published by Curious Publications
101 W. 23rd St. #318
New York, NY 10001
curiouspublications.com

Copyright © 2024

ISBN-13: 979-8-9914395-0-3

Originally published by the J. S. Ogilvie Publishing Company, 1915.
Cover image: *The Case For Spirit Photography*, Arthur Conan Doyle,
George H. Doran Company in 1923.
Inside cover images: National Media Museum Collection,
William Hope

Printed and bound in the United States of America.

A NOTE ON THE TEXT

Hereward Carrington (1880-1958) was one of the most fascinating psychical researchers of the early twentieth century. He studied numerous mediums, debunked many, but believed in others—particularly Eusapia Palladino. Carrington wrote extensively about his adventures with the Italian psychic in *Eusapia Palladino and Her Phenomena*, as well as other books. He also famously had an affair with Mina "Margery" Crandon, known as the Witch of Lime Street, in the 1920s.

Carrington's interest in the unusual led to a prolific writing career, including this title, which is a faithful reproduction of the original 1915 edition—including the advertisements at the back. The "Publisher's Note" that follows will offer more information about this unique author.

As for the *true* ghost stories found within these pages, well, they are true in that they are indeed ghost stories. But whether there's truth to the stories is for the reader to decide.

"TRUE GHOST STORIES"

But Not All Can Be Regarded as Verifiable

"True Ghost Stories," by Hereward Carrington (J. S. Ogilvie publishing company), puts on the cap and gown of science, but leaves the familiar face of superstition peeping out between.

The book is a collection of typical anecdotes about ghosts, chosen for their startling circumstances, and as such it can be read once with some interest; but it fails in its attempt to gain an air of solemn verity by such devices as frequent mention of the society for psychical research, and a glossary of terms such as "pact," "percipient" and "death-coincidence."

Its quality as science is shown by its including in a list of "historical ghosts" the mysterious man in black who ordered Mozart to compose a requiem. This ghost, though the book does not say so, was long ago found to be of the world and the flesh—one Leutgeb, a servant of Count von Wallsegg, who wished to publish the requiem as his own. Others of the "True Ghost Stories" are probably just as open to explanation.

Original newspaper review from the *Springfield Daily Republican* (Springfield, Massachusetts), January 11, 1916.

True Ghost Stories

BY
HEREWARD CARRINGTON

Author of "The Physical Phenomena of Spiritualism,"
"The Coming Science," "Death: its Causes and Phenomena,"
"Death Deferred," etc.

New York
The J. S. Ogilvie Publishing Company
57 Rose Street

Copyright, 1915, by
J. S. OGILVIE PUBLISHING COMPANY

To
MY DEAR FRIENDS
THE MARSHALLS

CONTENTS

BIOGRAPHICAL SKETCH	15
PREFACE	17
Glossary of Terms Used	19

CHAPTER I

What is a Ghost?	21
The Terror of the Dark	22
What is a Ghost?	25
Historic Investigations	26
Death Coincidences	28
Are They Due to Chance?	30
The Explanation	31
Experimental Apparitions	33
Telepathic Hallucinations	36
Ghosts Which Move Material Objects	40
Photographs of Ghosts	41
The "Double" and the Spiritual Body	43
What Happens at the Moment of Death	45
How the Soul May Leave the Body	48
Theories of Haunted Houses	51
The Ghosts of Animals	53
The Clothes of Ghosts	55
Telepathy from the Dead	57
The Psychic Atmosphere	58
Forms Created by Will	59
Physical Manifestations	60
Can Haunted Houses be "Cured"?	61

CONTENTS

CHAPTER II

Phantasms of the Dead—I	63
A Russian Ghost	63
Grasped by a Spirit Hand	68
"I Am Shot!"	70
"Heave the Lead!"	71
The Rescue at Sea	74
How Ghosts Influence Us	80
How a Ghost Warned the King	83
The Stains of Blood	86
Face to Face	88
"Julia, Darling!"	89
The Cut Across the Cheek	90
The Invisible Hand	92
The Apparition of the Radiant Boy	94
Fisher's Ghost	97
Harriet Hosmer's Vision	99
The Apparition of the Murdered Boy	101
The Ghost in Yellow Calico	104

CHAPTER III

More Phantasms of the Dead—II	108
Compacts to Appear after Death	108
Lord Brougham's Vision	110
The Tyrone Ghost	112
Dead or Alive!	115
The Scratch on the Cheek	120
A Ghost in Hampton Court	123
Half-Past One O'clock	130
My Own True Ghost Story	156

CONTENTS

CHAPTER IV

Haunted Houses	143
The Record of a Haunted House	144
Proofs of Immateriality	147
Conduct of Animals in the House	148
B—— House	149
Willington Mill	152
The Great Amherst Mystery	154
Brook House	162

CHAPTER V

Ghost Stories of a More Dramatic Nature	168
Disease-Phantoms	168
The Tale of a Mummy	171
Face Slapped by a Ghost	176
Alone with a Ghost in Church	179
A Haunted House in France	181
A Haunted House in Georgia	183
Shaken by a Ghost	189
The House and the Brain	190

APPENDIX A

Historical Ghosts	198

APPENDIX B

The Phantom Armies Seen in France	203

APPENDIX C

Bibliography	211

PUBLISHER'S NOTE.

HEREWARD CARRINGTON, author of "True Ghost Stories," is well known in this country, and in Europe, as a prominent scientific writer on psychical and occult subjects. He has been a member of both the English and American Societies of Psychical Research for more than 15 years; has written over a dozen books on the subject—a number of which has been translated into foreign languages (such as Japanese and Arabic), and he has lectured in London, Paris, Rome, Venice, Milan, Genoa, Turin, etc.—before scientific organizations. His writings are well known, and have earned him a high place in psychical circles. He's a late member of the Council of the American Scientific Society, of the American Geographical Society, and of the American Health League. He collaborated in the "American Encyclopædia," "The Standard Dictionary," etc. His experience in the investigation of psychical mysteries is unrivalled. He has travelled all over the country investigating "cases," spending nights in "haunted houses," and accounts of his investigations have appeared in the Reports of the various Psychical Societies, and also in his own publications.

In "True Ghost Stories," Mr. Carrington presents a number of startling cases of this character; but they are not the ordinary "ghost stories"—based on pure fiction, and having no foundation in reality. Here we have a well-arranged collection of incidents, all thor-

PUBLISHER'S NOTE

oughly investigated and vouched for, and the testimony obtained first-hand and corroborated by others. The chapter on "Haunted Houses" is particularly striking. The first chapter deals with the interesting question, "What is a Ghost?" and attempts to answer this question in the light of the latest scientific theories which have been advanced to explain these supernatural happenings and visitants. It is a book of absorbing interest, and cannot fail to grip and hold the attention of every reader—no matter whether he be a student of these questions, or one merely in search of hair-raising anecdotes and stories. He will find them here a-plenty!

PREFACE

THE following little book endeavors to bring together a number of "ghost stories" of the more startling and dramatic type,—but stories, nevertheless, which seem to be well authenticated; and which have been obtained, in most instances, at first hand, from the original witnesses; and often contain corroborative testimony from others who also experienced the ghostly phenomena. Some of these incidents, indeed, rise to the dignity of scientific evidence; others are less well authenticated cases,—but interesting for all that. These have been grouped in various Chapters, according to their evidential value. Chapters II. and III. contain well-evidenced cases, some of which have been taken from the *Proceedings* and *Journals* of the Society for Psychical Research (S. P. R.), or from *Phantasms of the Living*, or from other scientific books, in which narratives of this character receive serious consideration. Chapter V., on the contrary, contains a number of incidents which,—striking and dramatic as they are,—cannot be included in the two earlier Chapters, as presenting real evidence of Ghosts; but are published rather as startling and interesting ghost stories. Chapter IV., devoted to "Haunted Houses," contains brief accounts of the most famous Haunted Houses, and of the phenomena which have been witnessed within them. Appendix A gives a list of a few of the important "Historical Ghosts," Appendix B describes the "Phantom Armies" lately seen by the

— PREFACE —

Allied troops in France—while Appendix C lists a number of books of Ghost Stories which the interested reader may care to peruse. A short Glossary, at the beginning of the book, explains the meaning of certain terms used,—which are not, perhaps, ordinarily met with in books of this character.

In the Introductory Chapter, I have endeavored to explain, very briefly, the nature and character of Ghosts; what they *are*; and the various scientific theories which have been brought forward, of late years, to explain Ghosts. I hope that this may prove of interest to the reader; in case it does not do so, he is invited to "skip" directly to Chapter II., which begins our account of "True Ghost Stories."

I wish to express my thanks in this place to the Council of the English S. P. R. for special permission to quote and to summarize several striking cases here reproduced; also to Miss Estelle Stead, for permission to utilize several cases previously printed at length in Mr. Wm. T. Stead's collections of Ghost Stories.   H. C.

GLOSSARY OF TERMS USED

Agent—The person who, in thought-transference experiments, endeavors to impress his thoughts upon the "percipient" or "receiver."

Death-Coincidence—A case in which an apparition or other ghostly phenomenon has taken place, at the moment of the death of the person represented by the phantom.

Ghost—An apparition, a phantom. Some contend that all ghosts are "subjective" or purely mental (hallucinations); others that some ghosts are "objective"—that is, space-occupying entities, which exist apart from the seer, who sees them. These points will be found fully discussed in this book.

Hallucination—A mental experience, in which a phantom is seen, a voice heard, etc., when there is no real external cause for this seeing or hearing. Hallucinations are more complete than mere "illusions."

Pact—An agreement, entered into before death, between two persons, that, whichever one dies first, shall appear to the other one. These are here called "Pact Cases." [A Pact may also mean an agreement between a necromancer of some spirit-intelligence,

GLOSSARY

as in Magic; but the word is not used in that sense in this book.]

PERCIPIENT—The receiver of the telepathic or other message. The one who experiences the phenomenon.

PHANTASM—A phantom; an apparition; a "ghost." The word is more inclusive than any of the words suggested; and is used by preference, by most psychic students.

TELEPATHY—Mind-reading; thought-transference.

TRUE GHOST STORIES

CHAPTER I

WHAT IS A GHOST?

GHOSTS have been believed in by every nation, at every time and at every stage of the world's evolution. No matter where we may go, we find them stalking through the pages of history;[1] and even in our own cynical and materialistic age, we not only find "ghosts" still; but the evidence for their existence is stronger than ever! It is nonsense to say that "no sensible person believes in ghosts," because many thousands of them *do*. Why do they believe? Would they believe if they had no cause to do so?

The "terror of the dark," which we all have more or less, from which every child suffers (how intensely!) during its early years— a terror which is, to a certain extent, shared by animals and even insects—does all this signify nothing? Those who have looked into this question thoroughly, believe that there is, in every truth, a terrible reality justifying this instinctive fear; that evil and horrible things lurk about us in the still, weird hours of the night; that there are truly "powers and principalities" with which we often toy, without knowing or realizing the frightful dangers which result from this tampering with the unseen world. Yes; there is a true "tyranny of the dark." Phenomena and ghostly manifestations take place in darkness which would never occur in light; and which cease when a light is struck. All ghostly phenomena are associated with darkness, and the "wee small hours of the night."

All this is exemplified in the following interesting narrative, which I may entitle:

THE TERROR OF THE DARK

"All my life I have been afraid of the dark," said an acquaintance to me the other day, when we were discussing psychical matters. "I know that it is childish," he continued, "and I ought to have outgrown it years ago; but, as a matter of fact, I haven't. After all, isn't there some reason for the fears that we all feel, more or less, at that time?

Doesn't the Bible speak of 'the terrors of the Dark;' and are not all animals, and even insects, afraid of the dark—so much so that you cannot induce them to enter a dark place if they can help it? Light not only enables you to see what is around you; but it acts in a certain positive manner over 'the powers of darkness,' whatever they are, and prevents their operation. All spirit mediums will tell you that materialization and manifestations of that character cannot take place in the light; it prevents their occurrence. So, after all, as I said, isn't there some reasonable ground for one's fear at such times?"

I said nothing; but gazed into the fire. After all, were not his arguments somewhat impressive?

"But," continued my friend, "it is not altogether because of these speculative reasons that I fear the dark; it is because of a terrible experience I once had, and which has left me terror-struck, ever since, whenever I am left without light even for an instant. I will tell you the story, and let you judge for yourself.

"It was several years ago; in an old house we rented at that time, and from which we removed soon after the event I am about to relate. I was afraid of the dark, even then, and always left a night-light burning by the side of my bed when I went to sleep. One night I woke up, feeling the springs of the bed on which I was lying vibrate in a peculiar manner, impossible to describe.

"Looking up, I saw, standing by the side of my bed, a young man, dressed in rags, having a face ghastly white, and showing every indication of dissipation. He was regarding me intently.

"I shall never forget the shock I received on beholding that figure; not only because of the unexpected appearance; but because of the fact that I could perceive the opposite wall and furniture *through* the body. I knew at once that I beheld a spirit; and my blood ran cold at the thought. What I had dreaded all my life was at last fulfilled!

"My next thought was 'I am so glad the night-light is burning. What should I do if I were in darkness?'

As though the form read my thoughts, and was intent on torturing me to the limit of endurance, it leaned over, and the next instant had snuffed the candle! The phantom and I were alone in the black darkness!

"Words cannot describe my feelings at that instant. The blood froze in my veins, and the tongue clave to the roof of my mouth. I tried to speak, but could not. I only held out one hand as if to ward off the awful presence by pressing it away.

"The next instant I felt the bed-clothes gently turned down on the further side of the bed, and partly pulled off me. The springs of the bed were depressed, and I knew that the fearsome visitor was crawling into bed! It would lie down by my side; perhaps touch me; perhaps—who could tell? The agony of mind I experienced in those few moments I shall never forget! My only wonder is that my reason did not give way!

"Then a curious thing happened. Even in the state of mind, as I was then, I could perceive that the bed was gradually rising up again into its normal position. The weight upon it was growing less and less. Finally, it was again level, and I felt the bed clothes carefully replaced over me. The phantom had withdrawn!

"For hours I lay awake, not daring to move. After what seemed a century, the first faint shafts of light fell across the room, betokening the welcome morn. Finally glorious day broke. Glorious light! Hateful darkness! Cannot you see why I hate it so?"

But, fortunately, this evil and horrible side of ghost-land is not universal.

Ghosts do not always present themselves as so formidable and gruesome! Some of them prove helpful; others seem to wish to right a wrong; some even seem to have a sense of humor! So there are all sorts of ghosts, just as there are all sorts of people; and the variety is just as great in the one case as in the other.

WHAT IS A GHOST?

But, after all, what *is* a ghost? What do we mean by this? Where do ghosts live, and how? What do they do with themselves? How do they manifest? Why do they return? These are some of the questions which the average man asks himself—unless he totally disbelieves in them.

Most men, it is true, disbelieve in ghosts—unless they have had some experience to convince them to the contrary. Yet, after all, why should they? As Mr. W. T. Stead once remarked:

"Real Ghost Stories! How can there be real ghost stories when there are no real ghosts?

"But are there no real ghosts? You may not have seen one, but it does not follow that therefore they do not exist. How many of us have seen the microbe that kills? There are at least as many persons who testify that they have seen apparitions as there are men of science who have examined the microbe. You and I, who have seen neither, must perforce take the testimony of others. The evidence for the microbe may be conclusive, the evidence as to apparitions may be worthless; but in both cases it is a case of testimony, not of personal experience."

The average conception of a Ghost is probably somewhat as follows: That it is a thin, tall figure, wrapped in a sheet, walking about the house, clanking chains behind it, and scaring out of his wits anyone who sees it. According to this view, a ghost would be as material and substantial a thing as a buzz-saw or a lap-dog, and exists just as fully "in space." Such, however, is not the conception of the ghost which modern science entertains. Many investigators who have examined this question closely have come to the conclusion that ghosts *do* actually exist; but when we come to the more troublesome question: *What are they?* we are met at once with difficulties and disagreements. The recent scientific theories and explanations of the subject are complex and subtle; and necessitate a certain preliminary knowledge on the part of the student in order for him to understand them. I shall explain as briefly and clearly as possible exactly what these theories are. For the moment, I wish to speak, first of all, of the history of psychic investigation; and particularly that portion of it which deals with apparitions or "ghost hunting."

HISTORIC INVESTIGATIONS

Here and there, serious investigators have always existed. In the sixteenth century Dr. Glanvil pursued this study with great genius and patience; Dr. Johnson also was a firm believer in the reality of "ghosts"; Sir Walter Scott and others of his time were investigators, the famous Dr. Perrier wrote a treatise on apparitions, and similar investigations have been continued up to the present day. The first organized and systematic attempt to solve the problem, and to find out exactly *what ghosts are*, however, was made by the Society for Psychical Research (S. P. R.) in 1882. Practically all the investigations which have been carried on since then have led to important results.

Soon after the above mentioned Society was founded, and material began to be collected, it was found that many cases had to do with haunted houses, many with apparitions, but the greater number of them hinged around the one point—the coincidence of apparitions with the death of the persons represented. An apparition of a certain person would be seen in London, let us say; and some hours later a telegram would arrive, conveying the news that this person had just been killed. When the time was compared, it was found to agree exactly; the hour of the death and that of the apparition tallying to the minute.

Chance, you say? Perhaps so. *One* case of this character might be explained in such manner; but could *fifty*? Could a *hundred*? It became a question of statistics—of figures; these alone can answer our question.

Before considering these, however, let us give a few examples of cases of "death-coincidences," so that the reader may see the character of the evidence presented. He may then appreciate the value of a great mass of such evidence, when published *in extenso*.

DEATH-COINCIDENCES

The first case we take is from M. Flammarion's book, *The Unknown* (p. 108), and is as follows:

"My mother ... who lived in Burgundy, heard one Tuesday, between nine and ten o'clock, the door of the bedroom open and close violently. At the same time, she heard herself called twice—'Lucie, Lucie!' The following Tuesday, she heard that her uncle Clementin, who had always had a great affection for her, had died that Tuesday morning, precisely between nine and ten o'clock...."

In the following instance, the notification is in visual, instead of auditory form, and is taken from the *Proceedings*, S. P. R., Vol. X., pp. 213-14:

"About the 14th of September, 1882, my sister and I felt worried and distressed by hearing the 'death watch'; it lasted a whole day and night. We got up earlier than usual the next morning, about six o'clock, to finish some birthday presents for our mother. As my sister and I were working and talking together, I looked up, and saw our young acquaintance standing in front of me and looking at us. I turned to my sister; she saw nothing. I looked again to where he stood; he had vanished. We agreed not to tell any one....

"Some time afterwards we heard that our young acquaintance had either committed suicide or had been killed; he was found dead in the woods, twenty-four hours after landing. On looking back to my diary, I found that the marks I made in it corresponded to the date of his death."

The following case is reported in Podmore's *Apparitions and Thought Transference*, p. 265:

"The first Thursday of April, 1881, while sitting at tea with my back to the window, and talking with my wife in the usual way, I plainly heard a rap at the window, and, looking round, I said to my wife, 'Why, there's my grandmother,' and went to the door, but could not see anyone; and still feeling sure it was my grandmother, and, knowing that, though eighty-three years of age, she was very active and fond of a joke, I went round the house, but could not see anyone. My wife did not hear it. On the following Saturday, I had news that my grandmother died in Yorkshire about half an hour before the time I heard the rapping. The last time I saw her alive I promised, if well, I would attend her funeral; that was some two years before. I was in good health and had no trouble; age, twenty-six years. I did not know that my grandmother was ill.

"Rev. Matthew Frost."

Mrs. Frost writes:

"I beg to certify that I perfectly remember all the circumstances my husband has named, but I heard and saw nothing myself."

The following case is from *Phantasms of the Living*, Vol. II., p. 50:

"On February 26th, 1850, I was awake, for I was to go to my sister-in-law, and visiting was then an event for me. About two o'clock in the morning my brother walked into our room (my sister's) and stood beside my bed. I called to her, 'Here is ——.' He was at the time quartered at Paisley, and a mail-car from Belfast passed about that hour not more than a mile from our village.... He looked down on us most lovingly, and kindly, and waved his hand, and he was gone! I recollect it all as if it were only last night it occurred, and my feeling of astonishment, not at his coming into the room at all, but where he could have gone. At that very hour he died."

Mr. Gurney writes:

"We have confirmed the date of death in the Army List, and find from a newspaper notice that the death took place in the early morning, and was extremely sudden."

Cases such as the above could be multiplied into the hundreds; but it is not necessary. For our present purposes, the above samples will at least serve to show the character of these "death-coincidences," and how accurate and how numerous they often are.

ARE THEY DUE TO CHANCE?

The cases of "death-coincidences" came in so thick and so fast that, some time after its foundation, the Society for Psychical Research published an enormous book in two volumes, called "Phantasms of the Living," which contained some 702 cases of this character. The possibility of "chance coincidence" was very carefully worked out; and it was ascertained that the number of collected cases was many thousand times more numerous than chance alone could be supposed to account for. A "connection" of some sort was thought to be proved.

But objections at once began to be heard! "In order to prove your point you must collect a greater number of cases than this; you must get more facts before we can consider your point proved!"

So the investigators again set to work, and carried on a far more extensive investigation, in several countries, covering a period of several years. The results were the same. After collecting some 30,000 cases, and calculating the number of death-coincidences contained in this number, it was again proved, and most conclusively, that the number of coincidences was far more numerous than could be accounted for by any theory of chance. Professor Sidgwick's Committee, therefore, signed the following joint statement, at the conclusion of their lengthy Report:

"Between deaths and apparitions of the dying person a connection exists which is not due to chance alone. This we hold as a proved fact...."

These are weighty words. They represent an important forward step in our investigation of these involved and complex questions. *Something* takes place at death, which serves to unite, in some sort of spiritual bond, the dying and the still living relatives or friends. *What is* this connection? In what may it be supposed to consist?

THE EXPLANATION

For an explanation, we must begin by going back to experimental thought-transference. We know that it is possible, under certain conditions, for one person to affect another, otherwise than through the regular avenues of the five senses. This "telepathic" action between mind and mind is now pretty well known, and operates more or less throughout life. By means of this, it is occasionally possible for one person to impress a scene or a picture upon the mind of another, so that the other shall see before him, as it were, in space, a vivid mental picture of the scene in the other's mind.

This being so, it seems plausible to suppose that it might be possible to convey the impression or picture of *one's self* to another—since this may be supposed to be the most precise and best-known picture we have. Would it not be possible to think of one's own appearance so intensely as to cause a mental representation of it to appear before another person, distant some miles away?

Apparently this *has* been done, many times. "Experimental apparitions" of this character have frequently been *induced*; accounts of a few of which will be found in this volume. The picture is mental, in such a case; it is an imaginative creation; it is a hallucination,—although it was caused or created by another, distant mind. It was, it is true, a hallucination; but as it was induced by telepathy, we have for such apparitions the name of "telepathic hallucinations." It is this theory of "telepathic hallucinations" which is invoked to explain many of these cases of death-coincidences, or apparitions of the dying.

EXPERIMENTAL APPARITIONS

The following types of "experimental apparitions" are good examples of the ability to induce a phantasmal form at a distance.by "willing" to do so. As to the nature of this figure: there is as yet no unanimity of opinion—some authorities preferring to believe that such cases represent merely an extension of the power of thought-transference, known to us; others, on the contrary, contending that such cases prove the existence and travelling powers of the "astral" or "spiritual body." Of this, however, more later.

Here is a case of this nature, experienced by the English investigator, the Rev. William Stainton Moses, who corroborates the following account, which is furnished by the agent:—

"One evening I resolved to appear to Z., at some miles' distance. I did not inform him beforehand of the intended experiment, but retired to rest shortly before midnight, my thoughts intently fixed on Z., with whose rooms and surroundings I was quite unacquainted. I soon fell asleep, and woke next morning unconscious of anything having taken place. On seeing Z. a few days afterwards, I inquired: 'Did anything happen at your rooms on Saturday night?' 'Yes,' he replied, 'a great deal happened. I had been sitting over the fire with M., smoking and chatting. About 12:30 he rose to leave, and I let him out myself. I returned to the fire to finish my pipe, when I saw you sitting in the chair just vacated by him. I looked intently at you, and then took up a newspaper to assure myself that

I was not dreaming; but on laying it down I saw you still there. While I gazed, without speaking, you faded away.'"

In the case which follows, the initials only are used; but the writer of the account was known to the officers of the S. P. R., who vouched for the general trustworthiness of the writer:

"On a certain Sunday evening in November, 1881, having been reading of the great power which the human will is capable of exercising, I determined, with the whole force of my being, that I would be present in spirit in the front bedroom of the second floor of a house situated at 22 Hogarth Road, Kensington, in which room slept two young ladies of my acquaintance,—namely, Miss L. S. V. and Miss E. C. V., aged respectively twenty-five and eleven years. I was living at the time at 23 Kildare Gardens, at a distance of about three miles from Hogarth Road, and I had not mentioned in any way my intention of trying this experiment to either of the above ladies, for the simple reason that it was only on retiring to rest upon this Sunday night that I made up my mind to do so. The time at which I determined to be there was one o'clock in the morning; and I had a strong intention of making my presence perceptible. On the following Thursday I went to see the ladies in question, and, in the course of my conversation (without any allusion to the subject on my part), the elder one told me that on the previous Saturday night she had been much terrified by perceiving me standing by her bedside, and that she screamed when the apparition advanced towards her, and awoke her little sister, who also saw me.

"I asked her if she was awake at the time, and she replied most decidedly in the affirmative; and, upon my inquiring the time of the occurrence, she replied, 'About one o'clock in the morning.'

"This lady at my request wrote down a statement of the event, and signed it...."

Mr. Gurney (one of the authors of *Phantasms of the Living*) became deeply interested in these experiments, and requested Mr. B. to notify him in advance on the next occasion when he proposed to make his presence known in this strange manner. Accordingly, March 22d, 1884, he received the following letter:

"Dear Mr. Gurney:—I am going to try the experiment to-night of making my presence perceptible at 44 Morland Square, at 12 P. M. I will let you know the result in a few days.

Yours very sincerely, "S. H. B."

The next letter, which was written on April 3, contained the following statement, prepared by the recipient, Miss L. S. Verity:

"On Saturday night, March 22, 1884, at about midnight, I had a distinct impression that Mr. S. H. B. was present in my room, and I distinctly saw him, being quite awake. He came toward me and stroked my hair. I voluntarily gave him this information when he called to see me on Wednesday, April 2, telling him the time and the circumstances of the apparition without any suggestion on his part. The appearance in my room was most vivid and quite unmistakable."

Miss A. S. Verity also furnishes this corroborative statement:

"I remember my sister telling me that she had seen S. H. B. and that he touched her hair, before he came to see us on April 2."

The agent's statement of the affair is as follows:

"On Saturday, March 22, I determined to make my presence perceptible to Miss V. at 44 Morland Square, Notting Hill, at twelve midnight; and as I had previously arranged with Mr. Gurney that I should post him a letter of the evening on which I tried my next experiment (stating the time and other particulars) I sent him a note to acquaint him with the above facts. About ten days afterwards I called upon Miss V., and she voluntarily told me that on March 22, at twelve o'clock, midnight, she had seen me so vividly in her room (whilst wide awake) that her nerves had been much shaken, and she had been obliged to send for a doctor in the morning."

These cases will at least prove the possibility of such a thing as "experimental apparitions," and, explain them as we may, they are, at all events, most interesting and significant. They prove the reality of "telepathic phantasms"—of apparitions produced in another by the power of mind. This is, at least, the modern conception of the facts.

TELEPATHIC HALLUCINATIONS

How may the theory be said to work? How can a telepathic impulse from a distant mind cause a picture to appear in space, as it were, before the recipient? Here is the last word of modern science in this direction; here is the theory which has been advanced to explain puzzling cases of this character.

When we look at and see an object, the sight-centers of the brain are roused into activity; unless they are so aroused, we see nothing, and whenever they are so aroused, *no matter from what cause*, we have the sensation of sight. We *see*.

But we get no further than this; we do not reason about the thing seen, or analyze; or think to ourselves, "this is a red apple; I like red apples," etc. No, we only see or perceive the object. All the reasoning *about* the object takes place in the higher thought-centres of the brain. A diagram will, perhaps, help to make all this clear.

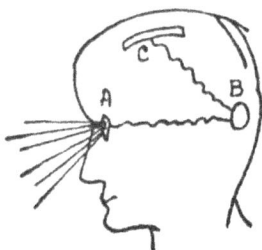

When light-waves coming from the eye, A, travel along the optic nerves, and excite into activity the sight-centers—at B—we have the sensation of sight, as before said. Nerve currents then travel *up* the nerves, going from B to C, and in these higher centers, they are associated and analyzed, and we then "reflect" upon the thing seen, etc. This is the normal process of sight.

Now, if the eye, or the optic nerves, or the

sight-centers themselves become diseased, we still have the sensation of seeing, though there is no material object there; we have ordinary hallucinations of all kinds—delirium tremens, etc. If the sight-centers are stimulated *as much* as they would be by the incoming nerve stimuli from the eye, we have "full-blown hallucinations."

Now, it is obvious that one method of stimulating the sight-centers into activity is for a nervous current to come *downwards*, along the nerves running from C to B. It is probable that something of this sort takes place when we experience "memory pictures." If you shut your eyes and picture the face of some dear friend, you will be able to see it before you more or less clearly. The higher psychical centers of the brain have excited the sight-centers into a certain activity; and these have given us the sensation of dim, inward sight. If the stimulus were stronger, we should have cases of intense "visualization"; such as the figures which occur in the crystal ball, etc.—they being doubtless produced in this manner.

Although the "sluice-gates," so to speak, running from C to B are, therefore, always open *slightly*; they are never open wide; it is not natural for them to be so. But if, under any great stress, thought or emotion, the downward nervous current were as strong as that ordinarily running from A to B; then we should appear to see as clearly; the object would appear just as solid and real and outstanding to us as any other entity. We should experience a "full-blown hallucination."

All this being so, it is almost natural to suppose

that *one* method by which these psychical sluice-gates could be more widely opened would be under the impact of *a telepathic impulse*. If we assume that this in some manner arouses into instantaneous and great activity the higher psychical centers (C), these would very probably communicate this impulse to B—downwards, along the nerve-tracts connecting the two (or to the hearing centers, when we should experience an auditory hallucination, and hear our name spoken, etc.). In this way we could account for a telepathic hallucination, originating in this manner; and it is surely to be supposed that, at the moment of death, some peculiar quickening of the mental and spiritual life takes place—the peculiar flashes of memory by those drowning, etc., seeming to show this.

So, then, we arrive at a sort of explanation of many of these cases of apparitions, occurring at the moment of death; for we have shown them to be "telepathic hallucinations." This is also the correct explanation, doubtless, for many cases in which apparitions of the living have been seen—in which a phantasm of a living person has appeared to another, during sleep, or in hypnotic trance, etc.

But how about those ghosts which appear some time after death? They, at least, cannot be explained by any such theory. What has been said by way of explanation of these cases?

It will be remembered that telepathy is the basis of the explanation thus far. Let us extend this. We have only to suppose that the spirit of man survives the shock of death, and that it can continue to exert its powers and capacities also. For, if a living mind can influence the living by telepathy; why not a "dead" one? Why should not the surviving spirit of man continue to influence us, by telepathy? If they could, we should still have cases of telepathic hallucinations—induced from the mind of a discarnate, not an incarnate, spirit. The "ghost" might still be a telepathic hallucination. And if several persons saw the figure at once, we should, on this theory, have a case of collective hallucination—in which one mind affected all the rest equally and simultaneously.

GHOSTS WHICH MOVE MATERIAL OBJECTS

Such is the theory—rather far-fetched, it is true; but certainly the most rational and common-sense so far advanced to explain many of the facts. It is probable, however, that this explanation will not serve to explain *all* of them. Thus, in those cases where the apparition moved a material object, opened a door, etc., such a theory would have to be abandoned, for the simple reason that a mental concept, an hallucination, cannot open doors and move objects! There must be an outstanding, material entity to effect this. There must be a real ghost. And in those cases where the apparition has been seen by several persons at once, or even photographed, it seems more reasonable to suppose that a material, space-occupying body was present rather than to assume that the various witnesses or the camera were hallucinated.

In the following cases, for example, the apparition

performs a definite physical action—snuffs a candle with its fingers, an action which a pure hallucination could hardly be supposed to perform. The account is by the Rev. D. W. G. Gwynne, M.I., and is printed in *Phantasms of the Living*, Vol. II., pp. 202-3. After telling of certain minor phenomena, he proceeds:

"I now come to the mutual experience of something that is as fresh in its impression as if it were the occurrence of yesterday. During the night I became aware of a draped figure passing across the foot of the bed towards the fireplace. I had the impression that the arm was raised, pointing with the hand towards the mantlepiece, on which a night-light was burning. Mrs. Gwynne at this moment seized my arm, and the light *was extinguished*. Notwithstanding, I distinctly saw the figure returning towards the door, and being under the impression that one of our servants had found her way into the room, I leaped out of bed to intercept the intruder, but found, and saw, nothing...."

[Mrs. Gwynne confirms the story, adding, "I distinctly saw the hand of the phantom placed over the night-light, which was at once extinguished."]

PHOTOGRAPHS OF GHOSTS

Again, it is claimed that ghosts have sometimes been photographed, though very rarely. In a number of cases, attempts have been made to photograph ghosts seen in haunted-houses; but, though the figures have been seen by all present, the photographic plate has failed to record any impression of the phantom. In other cases, on the contrary, definite impressions *have* been obtained; and, though there is doubtless much fraud among professional mediums, who claim to produce "spirit photographs," there are many cases on record in which no professional medium was employed, and in which faces were certainly seen upon the developed plate. Experiments have also been made in photographing the body at the moment of death; to see if any impression could be made upon the plate—by the soul, in its passage from the body; and, though many of these have proved negative, Dr. Baraduc, of Paris, has obtained a number of photographs which have never been explained. Again, numerous researches in the region of so-called "thought photography" have given some basis for the belief that thought may be, under certain conditions, photographed—as for example, in the experiments of Dr. Ochorowicz and others. It may be said, therefore, that some progress is being made in this direction by psychic investigators (particularly by the French observers, who are far ahead of the rest of the world in these branches of psychic investigation), and that, with increased sensitiveness of film and plate, and greater perfection of lens and camera, it is to be hoped that the time is not far distant when it will be possible to photograph the unseen just as we photograph living persons.

There are "ghosts," therefore, which are hallucinations; and there are ghosts which are genuine phantasms—the "real article." It becomes a question, in each instance, of sifting the evidence; finding out *which they are.* Yet, if there are real, objective, outstanding ghosts, how can we explain them? In what do they consist? In short, we are back to our original question: What are ghosts?

THE "DOUBLE," AND THE SPIRITUAL BODY

Before we can answer this question satisfactorily, we must consider one or two preliminary questions. First of all, we must speak of the "double"—the astral or spiritual or ethic body, which resides in man, as well as his physical body.[2]

St. Paul constantly emphasized the fact that man has a material body and a "spiritual body." This inner body is the exact shape of the physical body—its counterpart, its double. In life, under ordinary conditions, the two are inseparable; but at death, the severance takes place and man continues to live on in this etheric envelope. This inner body has been studied very carefully by students of the occult; and a good deal is now known about it—its comings and goings, its composition, and the method of its departure at death. For our present purposes, however, it is enough to say that such a body exists, and that it is the vehicle man continues to use and manipulate, after his death and his departure from this plane.

---

[2] Theosophists distinguish between all these various bodies; psychic students strive, for the most part, only to prove the objective existence of any one of them.

It so happens that, under certain peculiar conditions, the inner body of man is capable of being detached or separated from the physical body. This usually occurs in trance, sleep, hypnotic and mesmeric states, etc.; or may be performed "experimentally," by some who have cultivated this power in themselves. When this body goes on such "excursions"—leaving the physical body practically dead, to all appearances—it may be seen by those in its immediate vicinity, just as a material body would be—if they are sufficiently sensitive or receptive.

The following interesting case, (recorded in *Phantasms of the Living*, Vol. I, pp. 225-26) is a good example of the apparent traveling of the body to another place, and the perception of that body by a second person, who happens to be there. Two individuals, at all events, shared in the experience, which is otherwise hard to account for. The case is recorded by the Rev. P. H. Newnham, and is as follows:

"In March, 1854, I was up at Oxford, keeping my last term, in lodgings. I was subject to violent neuralgic headaches, which always culminated in sleep. One evening, about 8 p.m., I had an unusually violent one; when it became unendurable, about 9 p.m., I went into my bedroom, and flung myself, without undressing, on the bed, and soon fell asleep.

"I then had a singularly clear and vivid dream, all the incidents of which are as clear in my memory as ever. I dreamed that I was stopping with the family of a lady who subsequently became my wife. All the younger ones had gone to bed, and I stopped chatting to the father and mother, standing up by the fireplace. Presently I bade them good-night, took my candle, and went off to bed. On arriving in the hall, I perceived that my fiancee had been detained downstairs, and was only then near the top of the staircase. I rushed upstairs, overtook her on the top step, and passed my two arms around her waist, under her arms, from behind. Although I was carrying my candle in the left hand, when I ran upstairs, this did not, in my dream, interfere with this gesture.

"On this I woke, and the clock in the house struck ten almost immediately afterwards.

"So strong was the impression of the dream that I wrote a detailed account of it the next morning to my fiancee.

"*Crossing* my letter, *not* in answer to it, I received a letter from the lady in question: 'Were you thinking about me very specially last night, just about ten o'clock? For, as I was going upstairs to bed, I distinctly heard your footsteps on the stairs, and felt you put your arms round my waist.'"

[Mrs. Newnham wrote a confirmation of this account, which was also published.]

WHAT HAPPENS AT THE MOMENT OF DEATH

In all these cases, of course, the psychic body of the subject returns and re-animates the physical body; for if it did not do so, death would take place. When death does actually take place, this is what occurs; and psychics and clairvoyants assert that they are able to see and follow this process perfectly; and many of them have described exactly what takes place at the moment of death. The following description, for example, given by Andrew Jackson Davis, is taken from his *Death, and the After Life*, pp. 15-16, and is as follows:

"Suppose the person is now dying. It is to be a rapid death. The feet first grow cold. The clairvoyant sees over the head what may be called a magnetic halo—an etherial emanation, in appearance golden, and throbbing as though conscious. The body is now cold up to the knees and elbows, and the emanation has ascended higher in the air. The legs are cold to the hips and the arms to the shoulders; and the emanation, though it has not risen higher in the room, is more expanded. The death-coldness steals over the breast and round on either side, and the emanation has attained a higher position nearer the ceiling. The person has ceased to breathe, the pulse is still, and the emanation is elongated and fashioned in the outline of a human form. Beneath, it is connected with the brain. The head of the person is internally throbbing—a slow, deep throb—not painful but like the beat of the sea. Hence the thinking faculties are rational, while nearly every part of the person is dead. Owing to the brain's momentum, I have seen a dying person, even at the last feeble pulsebeat, rouse impulsively and rise up in bed to converse with a friend, but the next instant he was gone—his brain being the last to yield up the life principle.

"The golden emanation, which extends up midway to the ceiling, is connected to the brain by a very fine life-thread. Now the body of the emanation ascends. Then appears something white and shining, like a human head; next, in a very few moments, a faint outline of the face divine, then the fair neck and beautiful shoulders; then, in rapid succession, come all parts of the new body down to the feet—a bright, shining image, a little smaller than its physical body, but a perfect prototype or reproduction in all except its disfigurements. The fine life-thread continues attached to the old brain. The next thing is the withdrawal of the electric principle. When this thread snaps the spiritual body is free, and prepared to accompany its guardians to the Summer-Land. Yes, there is a spiritual body; it is sown in dishonor and raised in brightness."

It is doubtless this spiritual body which is the true cause of many apparitions—of many ghost stories. It is this body which is seen by the seer or percipient in many a ghost story; it is this body which moves objects and touches the individual who sees the ghost. This body is detached at death, as we have seen, and afterwards is free to rove at its own free will. Apparitions of the dead might thus be accounted for; while all those cases of apparitions of the dying which are with difficulty explained as due to pure telepathy might also thus find their explanation. The spiritual body, freed at that moment, would manifest its presence to the distant percipient as it did after death. So far so good, but how about apparitions of the living? How explain those cases in which the apparition of a living person has been seen, when the spiritual body is supposedly safely attached to the physical body?

Many of them are doubtless cases of telepathy; but in those cases which seem to demand the presence of a body of some sort, we may suppose that the spiritual body may become detached, at times, under certain peculiar conditions, from the material body which it inhabits and animates, and can then manifest independently at a distance. The following cases are illustrative, apparently, of this fact; showing us that the "etheric body" can manifest on occasion at will at a distance from the physical body.

HOW THE SOUL MAY LEAVE THE BODY

"... I put out the light and returned, but no sooner had I done this than ... I could feel a creeping sensation moving up my legs. I got up and lit the gas and went back to bed; with pillows arranged in such a way as to make me comfortable. In a comparatively short time, all circulation ceased in my legs, and they were as cold as those of the dead. The creeping sensation began in the lower part of the body, and that also became cold.... There was no sensation of pain or even of physical discomfort. I would pinch my legs with my thumb and finger, and there was no feeling or no indication of blood whatever. I might as well have pinched a piece of rubber so far as the sensation produced was concerned. As the movement continued upward, all at once there came a flashing of lights in my eyes and a ringing in my ears, and it seemed for an instant as though I had become unconscious. When I came out of this state, I seemed to be walking in the air. No words can describe the exhilaration and freedom that I experienced. At no time in my life had my mind been so clear and so free. Just then I thought of a friend who was more than a thousand miles distant. Then I seemed to be traveling with great rapidity through the atmosphere about me. Everything was light and yet it was not the light of the day or the sun, but, I might say, a peculiar light of its own, such as I have never known. It could not have been a minute after that I thought of my friends, before I was conscious of standing in a room where the gas-jets were turned up, and my friend was standing with his back toward me, but, suddenly turning and seeing me, said: 'What in the world are you doing here? I thought you were in Florida'—and he started to come toward me. While I heard the words distinctly, I was unable to answer. An instant later I was gone; and the consciousness of the memorable things that transpired that memorable night has never been forgotten. I seemed to leave the earth, and everything pertaining to it, and enter a condition of life of which it is absolutely impossible to give here any thought I had concerning it, because there was no correspondence to anything I had ever seen or heard or known of in any way. The wonder and the joy of it was unspeakable; and I can readily understand now what Paul meant when he said 'I knew a man, whether in the body or out of it I know not, who was caught up to the third heaven, and saw things which it is not possible (lawful) to utter.'

"In this latter experience there was neither consciousness of time nor of space; in fact, it can be described more as a consciousness of elastic feeling than anything else. It came to me after a time that I could *stay* there if I so desired, but with that thought came also the consciousness of the friends on earth and the duties there required of me. The desire to stay was intense, but in my mind I clearly reasoned over it—whether I should gratify my desire or return to my work on earth. Four times my thought and reason told me that my duties required me to return, but I was so dissatisfied with each conclusion that I finally said: 'Now I will think and reason this matter out once more, and whatever conclusion I reach I will abide by.' I reached the same conclusion, and had not much more than reached it when I became conscious of being in a room and looking down on a body propped up in bed, which I recognized as my own! I cannot tell what strange feelings came over me. This body, to all intents and purposes, looked to be dead. There was no indication of life about it, and yet here I was apart from the body, with my mind perfectly clear and alert, and the consciousness of another body to which matter of any kind offered no resistance.

"After what might have been a minute or two, looking at the body, I began to try and control it, and in a very short time all sense of separation from the physical body ceased, and I was only conscious of a directed effort toward its use. After what seemed to be quite a long time, I was able to move, got up from the bed, dressed myself, and went down to breakfast....

"I may add that the friend referred to as having been seen by me that night was also distinctly conscious of my presence and made the exclamation mentioned. We both wrote the next day, relating the experience of the night, and the letters corroborating the incident crossed in the post."

Such strange doings certainly tend to prove that the human spirit can leave its body and rove abroad, at times; and if this is the case, it shows us that our body is far more detachable than we usually suppose; and hence that it can probably continue to exist after the death of the physical body, when it is detached altogether. Once this is proved, all objection to the reality and existence of "objective" ghosts will have been done away with.

THEORIES OF HAUNTED HOUSES

If we grant that certain houses may be "haunted," in the sense that they may be the centers of influences and forces as yet unseen and unknown, the question is: How explain such cases? What hypotheses can we advance to explain cases of haunted houses, which will recognize the reality of the phantom witnessed therein, and attempt to explain them as rationally as possible? Four main theories have been advanced by way of explanation, which I shall briefly outline.

(1). There is the theory that the figures seen in

houses of this nature are genuine, outstanding entities—real beings, which are just as real, though less solid and tangible, as any of the living inhabitants of the house. This is, of course, the popular conception of the ghosts seen in haunted houses, and it must be admitted that such a theory covers and explains the facts more completely and fully than any other. There are also many facts telling in its favor. For instance, when two persons see a figure from different angles or viewpoints; and one describes it in profile, while the other describes it as presenting a full face likeness; and if this is the angle in each case from which a real figure would naturally be seen, this surely seems to indicate that a solid form of some sort was present.

Again, when three or four or more people see a figure at the same time, it is surely a strain upon our credulity to believe that a number of persons were similarly "hallucinated" at precisely the same time and in the same manner; and easier to believe that they all saw a figure at the same time, though in differing degrees of vividness and detail.

Thirdly, we have the evidence from photography. In some instances, these figures have been photographed; and though there is doubtless much fraud in this connection, there is evidence that, in certain cases, genuine photographs of this nature have been taken. This is discussed elsewhere in this volume, however.

Fourthly, we have the behavior of animals, in haunted houses. They often appear to see figures visible or invisible to others present at the time—bark at them, rub against them, stare at them, act as though terrified at what they see, etc. This will be noticed in many of the stories; and can be explained only with difficulty if we are to believe that the figures seen are merely hallucinations.

THE GHOSTS OF ANIMALS, ETC.

I have elsewhere spoken of the apparent ability of animals to see phantasmal forms and figures. The reverse of this is also true. Ghosts of animals have been seen—spectral dogs, cats, horses as well as human beings. These apparitions are very perplexing, and raise the question of the immortality of animals—a very vexed question, which has given rise to much discussion. Mr. H. Rider Haggard records the case of his own dog, whose apparition he saw at the very moment that the dog was killed by an express train some miles away. Did the animal succeed in affecting his master by telepathy? If not, why the coincidence? I myself have recorded a case in which a (real) cat spat at a phantom dog, seen independently by a clairvoyant, who had described it a few moments before to a group of spectators. Such cases are very interesting. They tend to prove that dogs, cats, horses and other animals also survive death—a conclusion which is certainly the most humane and logical to many minds.

In addition to these animal apparitions, there are also grotesque, horrible, monstrous and undefinable ghosts. One or two cases of this character are described in this book. Sometimes the "seer" sees something awful, but cannot describe in words what it is. Many of the phantoms of the imaginative type are of this character. Again, there are grave-yard ghosts; banshees, gnomes, elementals, pixies, fairies, brownies, nature-spirits, hobgoblins, sylphs, salamanders, dragons, vampires, wraiths, corpse-candles, and many other awful beings which have been described from time to time in the past. We need not consider these in a book of this character, however. But, to return to our argument for the objective reality of "ghosts."

Fifthly, we have those cases in which the apparition has produced a physical effect in the material world—snuffed a light, opened a door, pulled back the bed-curtains, etc. A hallucinatory figure could not do this. It has been suggested that all this is only a part of the hallucination, but when the thing is found to have been moved in reality, we must explain this somehow; for otherwise how did it change its place?

Sixthly, we have cases in which the same apparition has been seen by several separate and independent persons in the same room or house, and afterwards they have recognized the features of this person in a photograph shown them—the photograph of the person supposed to haunt that particular house. If we were to believe that a simple hallucination caused the figure, how account for this identification? Surely the theory is far-fetched!

For all these reasons, therefore, and others it would be possible to mention, there is much to be said in favor of this theory of haunted houses; the theory which says that the figures seen are real, semi-material entities.

THE CLOTHES OF GHOSTS

(2). The second view, opposed to that mentioned above, is this: Someone living in a house has experienced a hallucination, and then seen the same thing over and over again, by reason of auto-suggestion; or, if he moves away, and another tenant takes the house in turn, the thoughts of this second tenant are influenced, through thought-transference, by the first tenant, who broods and thinks over his experiences in the "haunted house," wonders whether the people now living in it are experiencing phenomena, etc. In this way, the minds of those living in the house are constantly influenced by thought-transference by living minds; and hallucinatory figures are produced in them, just as the picture of a playing card is induced in experimental thought-transference.

There are two things to be said in favor of such a theory. In the first place, we have the analogy which telepathic experiments give us, in which certain visual images are undoubtedly transmitted from one mind to another; and it is natural to assume that an extension of this same process might account for many of the phantasmal forms seen in haunted houses, as explained elsewhere.

In the second place, we immediately surmount the difficulty presented by the ghost's *clothes*. This is a stumbling-block to many investigators. However much we might believe that an etheric or astral or spiritual body might continue to persist after death, it is hard to believe that the clothes of the person who died also had "spiritual counterparts," and returned with him, to visit the earth and the scenes of former joys and miseries! We seldom read of a ghost without clothes; nude ghosts are not the fashion! Yet if we cannot believe this, how are we to explain this difficulty—and the fact that ghosts wear ghostly garments?

If the ghost were a hallucination, we could understand all this easily enough. The clothes were imaginary, just as the figure was; they formed part of the mental image, just like the figures seen in dreams, etc. This, therefore, is one very strong point in favor of this hypothesis; but if the ghost is a real, outstanding entity, how account for his clothes?

Several tentative explanations have been forthcoming. In the first place, it has been suggested that all ghosts are in reality partial "materializations" and that it is possible for a spirit to materialize and form drapery as well as solid flesh and bone. Both are a sort of condensation of matter, in varying degrees.

Again, it has been suggested that a spirit has the power to create objects by the power of will; by merely thinking and willing to do so. In this way, man would be a real creator, in a miniature scale, and certain analogies could be found for this in the material world. The returning spirit would desire to return clothed; and this very desire would create the fitting garb. Other theories have been advanced, but the above are the simplest and most intelligible, and are all we need consider at present.

All these difficulties, however, tell against the substantiality of ghosts; and in favor of this second theory of haunted houses.

TELEPATHY FROM THE DEAD

(3). The third theory which has been advanced, is an extension of the second. Thought-transference is still the agency invoked to explain the facts—but from the minds of dead, and not living persons. That is, assuming telepathy to be true, and possible between living minds; and assuming that individual consciousness survives the change called death; we can readily imagine that those who have "passed over" might affect and influence the living by thought-transference also, just as they did in life. On this theory, therefore, the ghost would still represent a hallucination; a mental or imaginary figure, and it would still be induced by telepathy from a distant mind; but that mind would be that of a so-called dead person. After death, we might suppose, this person would be thinking or dreaming over the past events; the scenes of his joys and sorrows; and these dreams would tend to influence the minds of those still living, and cause them to see the figures seen. The figures, on this theory, would be hallucinatory, but they would have a real, objective basis and starting-point for all that; and, as such, would represent the continued existence and activity on the part of the dead.

Against this ingenious theory may be urged all

those arguments which have been cited in favor of the materiality of apparitions.

THE PSYCHIC ATMOSPHERE

(4). A fourth theory is that which says that some *subtle psychic atmosphere* is present in certain houses; and that this "atmosphere" affects and influences all who live within them, just as their physical atmosphere would, only in a different manner and degree. Everyone has doubtless experienced this atmosphere in certain houses, if they are at all sensitive. They either "like" a house or "dislike" it—for no apparent reason. Some houses rest and refresh you; others irritate you, etc. This theory contends that every living human being is constantly giving off a peculiar vital emanation or aura or effluence; and that this charges-up or impregnates the material objects in his immediate neighborhood, which soak it up like a sponge, and retain it after being removed from its presence. It is because of this fact that articles presented to trance mediums often recall the person to whom they belonged; it is because of this that "psychometry" is possible—that is, the ability of some persons to give the past history of an object by merely handling it; and it is because of this that certain houses become so charged with this magnetic aura, or whatever it may be, that they remain "charged" for some time; and, in discharging, create psychic disturbances and impressions which are seen or experienced as phantasmal appearances.

The chief objection to this theory is that it is difficult to see how this general and impersonal "charging" process can create definite and clear-cut forms, possessing all the appearances of reality. Doubtless each theory contains much truth; and haunted houses represent, in many cases, a combination of *all* these causes, working together and combining into one complex and unfortunately ill-understood whole. It is the duty of the future to disentangle this maze, as best it can; and explain the various factors which go to make up a haunted house of this character.

FORMS CREATED BY WILL

(5). Besides these theories, another might be suggested, which has never so far been advanced, so far as I am aware. It is that the phantasmal forms seen in haunted houses are real substantial *creations*, manufactured by the thoughts or will of the discarnate spirit, who fashions it out of "such stuff as dreams are made of." It has been said that "thoughts are things," and many believe that this is literally true. Certain it is that a limited number of peculiarly constructed persons can produce phenomena which seem to be solid creations of the will. So, if thought could ever be proved to be really creative; if it could not only *formulate* but *objectify* and *project into space* images and forms, we should have here a rational explanation of many ghosts, as well as of their behavior. And just here a few words as to this latter may not be out of place.

It has often been objected that ghosts cannot be realities; they cannot be real spirits, for the reason that they act in such a senseless manner. They seldom speak or reply, when spoken to. They seldom have any definite purpose. In short, they betray no intelligence. This being so, they must be hallucinations and not the realities they claim to be!

The answer to this objection is found in the following consideration. Even granting all this to be true, many believing in ghosts do not for an instant contend that such ghosts represent the actual person the figure symbolises. It is a mere projection; a shell; a form created by the discarnate spirit, a resemblance, a phantasm. The central consciousness which animated and still animates that person is not *in* the ghostly form, but elsewhere. The phantasm represents, merely, a sort of impersonal wraith, and, as such, cannot be expected to possess intelligence or human characteristics. None are present within it. It is a very different thing from the real person it represents. The insipid and unintelligent behavior of ghosts, therefore, is only what we should expect. This fact is no argument against their reality, when rightly understood and interpreted.

PHYSICAL MANIFESTATIONS

In addition to haunted houses of this type, there are others, which must be referred to very briefly. Thus, in some cases, no figures have been seen, but remarkable sounds have been heard—sounds which have never been accounted for. Bangs, knocks, monotonous reading aloud, whispering, footsteps, etc., are some of the noises and sounds which have been heard in this way, and their origin often remains a mystery. It would take too long to discuss the various explanatory theories which have been advanced by psychic students to account for these sounds.

In other types of haunted houses, physical manifestations take place, though nothing unusual is either seen or heard. Thus, in one case recorded by Lombroso (*After Death: What?*) numbers of bottles were broken one after the other, for no apparent cause, when he was actually looking at them. In still other cases, furniture has been upset, crockery broken, doorbells rung, etc., by no visible agency. John Wesley was persecuted in this manner for several years; and the reason was never discovered. Such cases are technically known as "poltergeists," and may be found in abundance in the "history of the supernatural."

CAN HAUNTED HOUSES BE "CURED"?

One question of considerable interest remains. It is this: Can so-called Haunted Houses be *cured*? Many of those who live in houses of this character would like to have these influences removed; but are unable to rid themselves of them. Can this be done?

In some cases, this has doubtless been accomplished; while in others it has failed. We know too little as yet to lay down any arbitrary laws or rules which may be followed with safety in cases of this character. Sometimes one method succeeds, while another fails. I have known of cases where "exorcism" worked a complete cure; of others in which it failed miserably. I have known of cases in which suggestion, rightly applied, rid the house of its ghost; in other instances, no result was produced by similar methods! In a few instances mediums and psychics have been able to assist; in others their presence only seemed to make matters worse. We can but experiment and learn. Those who may be more interested in this aspect of the question will find it treated in Chapter XV. of my book "*The Coming Science*," which is devoted to "Haunted Houses and their Cure."

CHAPTER II

PHANTASMS OF THE DEAD—I.

In the following Chapter, I shall give a number of cases in which "Ghosts," or "Phantasms of the Dead," as they are called, have appeared to one or more persons at one time; sometimes telling them something they did not know; sometimes moving material objects in the room; sometimes pulling the bed-clothes off, etc. Nearly all these cases are well authenticated, and have been narrated at first-hand. Many of them have the corroborative testimony of several other persons, who also saw the phantasmal figure, or in some way shared in the experience. I shall begin with—

A RUSSIAN GHOST

The following story is vouched for by Mr. W. D. Addison, of Riga, and sent by him to Mr. W. T. Stead, who published it in *Borderland*:

"It was in February, 1884, that the incidents I am about to relate occurred to me, and the story is well-known to my immediate friends.

"Five weeks previously my wife had presented me with our first baby, and our house being a small one, I had to sleep on a bed made up in the drawing room—a spacious but cozy apartment, and the last place in which one would expect ghosts to select for their wanderings.

"On the night in question I retired to my couch soon after ten, and fell asleep almost the moment I was between the sheets.

"Instead of sleeping as, I am thankful to say, is my habit, straight through till morning, I woke up after a short dreamless sleep with the dim consciousness upon me that some one had called me by name. I was just turning the idea over in my mind when all doubts were solved by my hearing my name pronounced in a faint whisper, 'Willy.' Now the nurse who was in attendance on the baby, and who slept in the dressing room adjoining our bedroom, had been ill for the past few days, and on the previous evening my wife had come and asked me to assist her with the baby. As soon, therefore, as I heard this whisper, I turned round thinking, 'Ah, it is the baby again.'

"The room had three windows in it, the night was moonless but starlit; there was snow on the ground, and therefore, 'snowlight,' and the blinds being up the room was by no means dark.

"The first thing I noticed on turning round was the figure of a woman close to the foot of the bed, and whom (following the bent of my thoughts) I supposed to be my wife. 'What is up?' I asked, but the figure remained silent and motionless, and my eyes being more accustomed to the dimness, I noticed that it had a gray looking shawl over its head and shoulders, and that it was too short in stature to be my wife. I gazed at it silently, wondering who it could be; apparitions and ghosts were far from my thoughts, and the mistiness of the outlines of this silent figure did not strike me at the moment as it did afterwards.

"I again addressed it, this time in the language of the country, 'What do you want?' Again no answer. And now it occurred to me that our servant girl sometimes walked in her sleep, and that this was she. Behind the head of my bed stood a small table, and I reached round for the match-box which was on it, never removing my eyes from the supposed somnambulist. The match-box was now in my hands, but just as I was taking out a match, the figure, to my astonishment, seemed to rise up from the floor, and move backwards toward the end window; at the same time it faded rapidly and became blurred with the gray light streaming in at the window, and 'ere I could strike the match it was gone. I lit the candle, jumped out of bed and ran to the door: it was fastened! To the left of the drawing room there was a boudoir, separated only by a curtain, this room was empty too, and the door likewise fastened.

"I rubbed my eyes. I was puzzled. It struck me now for the first time that the figure was hazy looking, also that my wife was the only person who called me 'Willy,' and certainly the only person who could give the word its English pronunciation. I first searched both drawing room and boudoir, and then, opening the door, stepped into the passage, and went to my wife's door and listened. The baby was crying and my wife was up, so I knocked and was admitted. Knowing her to be strong minded and not nervous, I quietly related my experience. She expressed astonishment, and asked if I was not afraid to return to my bed in the drawing room. However, I was not, and after chatting for a few moments went back to my quarters, fastened the door, and getting into bed, thought the whole matter over very quietly. I could think of no explanation of the occurrence, and, feeling sleepy, blew out the light and was soon sound asleep again.

"After a short but sound and dreamless slumber, I was again awakened, this time with my face towards the middle window; and there, close up against it, was the figure again, and owing to its propinquity to the light, it appeared to be a very dark object.

"I at once reached out for the matches, but in doing so upset the table, and down it went with my candlestick, my watch, keys, etc., making a terrific crash. As before, I had kept my eyes fixed on the figure, and I now observed that, whatever it was, it was advancing straight towards me, and in another moment retreat to the door would be cut off. It was not a comfortable idea to cope with the unknown in the dark, and in an instant I had seized the bed-clothes, and grasping a corner of them in each hand, and holding them up before me, I charged straight at the figure. (I suppose I thought that, by smothering the head of my supposed assailant, I could best repel the coming attack.)

"The next moment I had landed on my knees on a sofa by the window with my arms on the window-sill, and with the consciousness that 'it' was now behind me—I having passed through it. With a bound I faced round, and was immediately immersed in a darkness impalpable to the touch, but so dense that it seemed to be weighing me down and squeezing me from all sides. I could not stir; the bed-clothes which I had seized as described hung over my left arm, the other was free, but seemed pressed down by a benumbing weight. I essayed to cry for help, but realized for the first time in my life what it means for the 'tongue to cleave to the roof of the mouth'; my tongue seemed to have become dry and to have swelled to a thickness of some inches; it stuck to the roof of my mouth, and I could not ejaculate a syllable. At last, after an appalling struggle, I succeeded in uttering, and I know that disjointed words, half prayer, half execrations of fear, left my lips, then my mind seemed to make one frantic effort, there seemed to come a wrench like an electric shock and my limbs were free; it was as tho' I tore myself out of something. In a few seconds I had reached and opened the door and was in the passage, listening to the hammerings of my heart-beats. All fear was gone from me, but I felt as though I had run miles for my life and that another ten yards of it would have killed me.

"I again went to the door of my wife's room, and, hearing that she was up with the baby, I knocked and she opened. She is a witness to the state I was in: the drops rolling down my face, my hair was damp, and the beatings of my heart were audible some paces off. I can offer no explanations of what I saw, but as soon as my story became known, the people who had occupied the house previously told me that they had once put a visitor in that same drawing room, who had declared the room to be haunted and had refused to stay in it...."

GRASPED BY A SPIRIT HAND

The following account is vouched for by Major C. G. MacGregor, Ireland, who writes as follows:

"In the end of the year 1871 I went over from Scotland to pay a short visit to a relative living in a square on the north side of Dublin.

"In January, 1872, the husband of my relative, then in his eighty-fourth year, was seized with paralysis, and, having no trained nurse, the footman and I sat up with him for sixteen nights during his recovery. On the seventeenth night, at about 11:30 p.m., I said to the footman: 'The master seems so well, and sleeping soundly, I shall go to bed; and if he awakes worse, or you require me, call me.' I then retired to my room, which was over the one occupied by the invalid.

"I went to bed and was soon asleep, when some time afterwards I was awakened by a slight push on the left shoulder. I was at the time lying on my right side facing the door (which was on the right side of my bed, and the fireplace on the left). I started up and said: 'Edward, is there anything wrong?' I received no answer, but immediately received another push. I got annoyed and said, 'Can you not speak, man, and tell me if anything is wrong?' Still no answer; and I had a feeling that I was going to get another push when I suddenly turned around and caught (what I then thought) a human hand, warm, soft and plump. I said: 'Who are you?' but I got no answer. I then tried to pull the person towards me, to endeavor to find out who it was, but although I am nearly thirteen stone, I could not move whoever it was, but felt that I myself was likely to be drawn from the bed. I then said, 'I will know who you are,' and having the hand tight in my hand, with my left I felt the wrist and arm—enclosed, as it seemed to me, in a tight sleeve of some winter material with a linen cuff; but when I got to the elbow all trace of the arm ceased! I was so astonished that I let the hand go, and just then the house clock struck 2 a.m. I then thought no one could possibly get to the door without my catching them; but lo! the door was fast shut as when I came to bed, and another thought struck me—the fact that, when I pulled the hand, I heard no one breathing, though I myself was 'puffed' from the strength I used!

"Including the mistress of the house, there were in all five females, and I am assured that the hand belonged to no one of them. When I related the adventure, the servants exclaimed, 'Oh, it must be the master's old aunt Betty,'—an old lady who had lived for many years in the upper part of the house, occupying two rooms, and had died over fifty years ago, at a great age. I afterwards learned that the *room* in which I felt the hand had been considered 'haunted,' and many curious noises and peculiar incidents had occurred there, such as the bed-clothes being torn off. One lady got a slap in the face from some invisible hand, and, when she lighted her candle, she saw something opaque fall, or jump off the bed. A general officer, a brother of the lady, slept there two nights, but preferred going to an hotel rather than remaining a third! He never would say what he heard or saw, but always asserted the room was 'uncanny.' I slept for months in that room afterwards and was never in the least disturbed. I never knew what nervousness was in my life, and only regret that my astonishment caused me to let go the hand before finding out the purpose of the visit. Whether it was meant for a warning or not, I may add that the old gentleman lived three years and six months afterwards...."

"I AM SHOT!"

The next case is well authenticated, and appeared in the *Proceedings* of the Society for Psychical Research (S. P. R.):

After some preliminary remarks, the writer proceeds:

"I awoke and saw standing by my bed, between me and the chest of drawers, a figure, which, in spite of the unwonted dress—unwonted, at least, to me—and of a full, black beard, I at once recognized as that of my old brother officer. He had on the usual khaki coat, worn by the officers on service in eastern climates.... His face was pale, but his bright black eyes shone as keenly as when, a year and a half before, they had looked upon me as he stood with one foot on the hansom, bidding me *adieu*.

"Fully impressed for the moment that we were stationed together in Ireland or somewhere, and thinking I was in my barrack-room, I said, 'Hello, P., am I late for parade?' P. looked at me steadily, and replied, 'I'm shot!'

"'Shot!' I exclaimed, 'Good God, how and where?'

"'Through the lungs,' replied P.; and as he spoke his right hand moved slowly up to his breast, until the fingers rested over the right lung.

"'What were you doing?' I asked.

"'The General sent me forward,' he answered; and the right hand left the breast to move slowly to the front, pointing over my head to the window, and at the same moment the figure melted away. I rubbed my eyes, to make sure I was not dreaming, and sprang out of bed. It was then 4.10 a.m. by the clock on my mantelpiece.

"Two days later news was received that he had been killed at Lang's Neck between 11 and 12 o'clock on the night in question."

The following is a nautical story:

HEAVE THE LEAD!

In the year 1664, Captain Thomas Rogers, commander of a ship called the *Society*, was bound on a voyage from London to Virginia. The vessel being sent light to Virginia, for a loading of tobacco, carried little freight in her outward hold.

"One day when they made an observation, the mates and officers brought their books and cast up their reckonings with the captain, to see how near they were to the coast of America. They all agreed that they were a *hundred leagues* from the capes of Virginia. Upon these customary reckonings, and heaving the lead, and finding no ground at a hundred fathoms, they set the watch, and the captain turned in.

"The weather was fine; a moderate gale of wind blew from the coast; so that the ship might have run about twelve or thirteen leagues in the night, after the captain was in his cabin.

"He fell asleep, and slept very soundly for about three hours, when he woke again, and lay still till he heard his second mate turn out and relieve the watch. He then called his first mate, as he was going off watch, and asked him how all things fared? The mate answered that all was well, though the gale had freshened, and they were running at a great rate; but it was a fair wind, and a fair, clear night.

"The captain then went to sleep again.

"About an hour after, he dreamed that some one had pulled him, and bade him turn out and look abroad. He, however, lay still and went to sleep again; but was suddenly re-awakened. This occurred several times; and, though he knew not what was the reason, yet he found it impossible to go to sleep any more. Still he heard the vision say: 'Turn out and look abroad.'

"The captain lay in this state of uneasiness nearly two hours, until finally he felt compelled to don his great coat and go on deck. All was well; it was a fine, clear night.

"The men saluted him; and the captain called out: 'How's she heading?'

"'Southwest by south, sir,' answered the mate; 'fair for the coast, and the wind east by north.'

"'Very good,' said the captain, and as he was about to return to his cabin, *something* stood by him, and said: 'Heave the lead.'

"Upon hearing this the captain said to the second mate: 'When did you heave the lead? What water had you?'

"'About an hour ago, sir,' replied the mate; 'sixty fathom.'

"'Heave again,' the captain commanded.

"When the lead was cast they had ground at eleven fathoms. This surprised them all; but much more when, at the next cast, it came up *seven* fathoms.

"Upon this, the captain, in a fright, bid them put the helm alee, and about ship, all hands ordered to back the sails, as is usual in such cases.

"The proper orders being observed, the ship 'stayed' and came about; but before the sails filled, she had but four-fathoms-and-a-half water under her stern. As soon as she filled and stood off, they had seven fathoms again, and at the next cast eleven fathoms, and so on to twenty fathoms. They then stood off to seaward all the rest of the watch, to get into deep water, till daybreak, when, being a clear morning, the capes of Virginia were in fair view under their stern, and but a few leagues distant. Had they stood-on but one cable-length further, as they were going, they would have been ashore, and certainly lost their ship, if not their lives—all through the erroneous reckonings of the previous day. *Who* or *what* was it that waked the captain and bade him save the ship? That he has never been able to tell!"

The incident which follows is somewhat similar—though more dramatic—being also a nautical story:

THE RESCUE AT SEA

The following famous narrative is taken from Mr. Robert Dale Owen's collection, printed in his *Footfalls on the Boundary of Another World*, and *The Debatable Land Between this World and the Next*. It is quite a famous case, and is vouched for by Mr. Owen. It is as follows:

"Mr. Robert Bruce, descended from some branch of the Scottish family of the same name, was born in humble circumstances about the close of the eighteenth century at Torbay, in the south of England, and there bred up to a seafaring life. When about thirty years of age (in the year 1828), he was first mate on board a barque trading between Liverpool and St. John's, New Brunswick.

"On one of her voyages, bound westward, being then some five or six weeks out, and having neared the eastern portion of the Banks of Newfoundland, the captain and the mate had been on deck at noon, taking an observation of the sun; after which they both descended to calculate their day's work.

"The cabin, a small one, was immediately at the stern of the vessel, and the short stairway, descending to it, ran athwart-ships. Immediately opposite to this stairway, just beyond a small, square landing, was the mate's state room; and from that landing there were two doors, close to each other—the one opening aft into the cabin, the other fronting the stairway into the stateroom. The desk in the stateroom was in the forward part of it, close to the door; so that anyone sitting at it, and looking over his shoulder, could see into the cabin.

"The mate, absorbed in his calculation, which did not result as he expected, varying considerably from the 'dead reckoning,' had not noticed the captain's motions. When he had completed his calculations, he cried out, without looking round, 'I make our latitude and longitude so-and-so. Can that be right? How is yours, sir?'

"Receiving no reply he repeated the question, glancing over his shoulder and perceiving, as he thought, the captain busy at his slate. Still no answer! Thereupon he rose, and, as he fronted the cabin door, the figure he had mistaken for the captain raised his head and disclosed to the astonished mate the features of an entire stranger.

"Bruce was no coward, but as he met that fixed gaze, looking directly at him in grave silence, and became assured that it was no one whom he had ever seen before, it was too much for him; and, instead of stopping to question the seeming intruder, he rushed upon deck in such evident alarm that it instantly attracted the captain's attention.

"'Why, Mr. Bruce,' said the latter, 'what in the world is the matter with you?'

"'The matter, sir? Who is that at your desk?'

"'No one that I know of.'

"'But there *is*, sir, there's a stranger there.'

"'A stranger? Why, man, you must be dreaming! You must have seen the steward there, or the second mate. Who else would venture down without orders?'

"'But, sir, he was sitting in your arm chair, fronting the door, writing on your slate. Then he looked up full in my face; and if ever I saw a man plainly and distinctly in the world I saw him.'

"'Him! Who?'

"'Heaven knows, sir; I don't! I saw a man and a man I have never seen in my life before.'

"'You must be going crazy, Mr. Bruce. A stranger, and we nearly six weeks out!'

"The captain descended the stairs, and the mate followed him. Nobody in the cabin! They examined the staterooms. Not a soul could be found.

"'Well, Mr. Bruce,' said the Captain, 'did not I tell you that you had been dreaming?'

"'It's all very well to say so, sir; but if I didn't see that man writing on the slate may I never see home and family again!'

"'Ah! Writing on the slate. Then it should be there still!' And the captain took it up. 'By heaven,' he exclaimed, 'here's something sure enough! Is that your writing, Mr. Bruce?'

"The mate took the slate; and there, in plain, legible characters, stood the words: 'Steer to the Nor'-west.'

"The captain sat down at his desk, the slate before him, in deep thought. At last turning the slate over, and pushing it toward Bruce, he said: 'Write down: "Steer to the nor'west."'

"The mate complied; and the captain, comparing the two handwritings, said: 'Mr. Bruce, go and tell the second mate to come down here.'

"He came, and at the captain's request, he also wrote the words. So did the steward. So in succession did every man of the crew who could write at all. But not one of the various hands resembled, in any degree, the mysterious writing.

"When the crew retired, the captain sat deep in thought. 'Could anyone have been stowed away?' at last he said. 'The ship must be searched. Order up all hands.'

"Every nook and corner of the vessel was thoroughly searched; not a living soul was found.

"Accordingly, the captain decided to change the vessel's course according to the instructions received. A look-out was posted; who shortly reported an iceberg, and then, shortly after, a vessel close to it.

"As they approached, the captain's glass disclosed the fact that it was a dismantled ship, apparently frozen to the ice.... It proved to be a vessel from Quebec, bound for Liverpool, with passengers on board. She had got entangled in the ice, and finally frozen fast; and had passed several weeks in a most critical situation. She was stove, her decks swept; in fact, a mere wreck; all her provisions and almost all her water gone. Her crew and passengers had lost all hope of being saved, and their gratitude at the unexpected rescue was proportionately great.

"As one of the men who had been brought away in the third boat ascended the ship's side, the mate, catching a glimpse of his face, started back in consternation. It was the very face he had seen three or four hours before, looking up at him from the captain's desk! He communicated this fact to the captain.

"After the comfort of the passengers had been seen to, the captain turned to the stranger, and said to him: 'I hope, sir, you will not think I am trifling with you, but I would be much obliged to you if you would write a few words on this slate.' And he handed him the slate, with that side up on which the mysterious writing was not.

"'I will do anything you ask,' replied the passenger, 'but what shall I write?'

"'A few words are all I want. Suppose you write: 'Steer to the nor'-west.'

"The passenger, evidently puzzled to make out the motive of such a request, complied, however, with a smile. The captain took up the slate and examined it closely; then stepping aside so as to conceal the slate from the passenger, he turned it over and gave it to him the other side up.

"'You say that this is your handwriting?' said he.

"'I need not say so,' replied the other, looking at

it, 'for you saw me write it.'

"'And this?' said the captain, turning the slate over.

"The man looked first at one writing, then at the other, quite confounded. At last: 'What is the meaning of this?' said he. 'I only wrote *one* of these. Who wrote the *other*?'

"'That's more than I can tell you, sir. My mate here says you wrote it, sitting at this desk, at noon to-day!'

"The captain of the wreck and the passenger looked at each other, exchanging glances of intelligence and surprise; then the former asked the latter: 'Did you dream that you wrote on this slate?'

"'No, sir, not that I remember.'

"'You speak of dreaming,' said the captain of the barque. 'What was this gentleman about at noon to-day?'

"'Captain,' rejoined the other, (the captain of the wreck), 'the whole thing is most mysterious and extraordinary; and I had intended to speak to you about it as soon as we got a little quiet. This gentleman—pointing to the passenger—being much exhausted, fell into a heavy sleep, or what seemed such, some time before noon. After an hour or more, he awoke, and said to me: 'Captain, we shall be relieved this very day.' When I asked him what reason he had for saying so, he replied that he had dreamed that he was on board a barque, and that she was coming to our rescue. He described her appearance and rig, and, to our utter astonishment, when your vessel hove in sight, she corresponded exactly to his description of her!

We had not put much faith in what he said; yet still we hoped there might be something in it, for drowning men, as you know, catch at straws. As it turned out, I cannot doubt that it was all arranged by some overruling Providence.'

"'There is not a doubt,' replied the captain of the barque, 'that the writing on the slate, let it come there as it may, saved all your lives. I was steering at the time considerably south of west, and I altered my course for the nor'-west, and had a look-out aloft, to see what would come of it. But you say,' he added, turning to the passenger, 'that you did not dream of writing on a slate?'

"'No, sir. I have no recollection whatever of doing so. I got the impression that the barque I saw in my dream was coming to rescue us; but *how* that impression came I cannot tell. There is another very strange thing about it,' he added. 'Everything here on board seems to be quite familiar; yet I am very sure that I was never in your vessel before. It is all a puzzle to me! What did your mate see?'

"Thereupon Mr. Bruce related to them all the circumstances above detailed."

HOW GHOSTS INFLUENCE US

The following is a very interesting case, which brings vividly before us the fact that ghosts often draw power from those who witness their manifestations—just as they draw vitality from a materializing "medium," during a seance. As cases of this character are rare, the following is of considerable value:

"It was an afternoon, last autumn, about six o'clock. I had returned from a stroll and was sitting in my own apartment on Central Park West, reading *Vanity Fair*. While turning over its pages I became suddenly aware of a novel and indescribable sensation. My chest and breathing became inwardly oppressed by some ponderous weight, while I became conscious of some 'presence' behind me, exerting a powerful influence on the forces within. On trying to turn my head to see what it could be, I was powerless to do so; neither could I lift a hand, or move in any way. I was not a little alarmed, and began immediately to reason. My mind was alive, though physically I was unable to move a muscle. It was as if the current of nerve force within seemed forcibly drawn together and focussed on a spot in front of me.

"I gazed motionless, as though with something intenser than ordinary eyesight, on what was no longer vacant space. There an oval, misty light was forming—elongatory, widening, yes, actually developing into a human face and form. Was this hallucination, or some vision of the unseen, coming in so unexpected a fashion? Before me had arisen a remarkable figure, never seen before in a picture or life—dark-skinned, aged, with white beard, the expression intensely earnest, the features small, the bald head finely moulded, lofty over the forehead, the whole demeanor instinct with solemn grace.

"He was speaking to me in deep tones, as if in urgent entreaty. What would I not give to hear words from such a figure! But no effort availed me to distinguish one articular sound. I tried to speak, but could not. With desperate effort I shook out the words, 'Speak louder.' The face grew more intent, the voice louder and more emphatic. Was there something amiss with my own hearing, then, that I could distinguish no word amid these deeply emphasized tones? Slowly and deliberately the figure vanished—through the same stages of indistinctness, back to the globular lamplike whiteness, till it faded to nothingness. Before it had quite faded away, the face only of a woman arose, indistinct and dim. The same emphatic hum, though in a subdued note; the same paralysis of voice and muscle, the same strange force, as it was overshadowing me. With the disappearance of this second and far less interesting figure, I recovered my power of movement and arose.

"My first impulse was to look around for the origin of this strange force; my second to rush to the looking-glass to make sure of myself. There could be no illusion. There I was, paler than usual, the forehead bathed in perspiration. I threw open the window. It was no dream. There were the passing trolley cars below, clanging up and down, while a crowd of noisy youngsters were playing in the park across the way. I sponged my face, and, greatly agitated, walked hurriedly to and fro. If this is real, I thought, it may recur. I would sit in the same position, try to be calm, read a book, remain as still and passive as I could, and see the result.

"To my intense interest, and almost at once,

the strange sense of some power operating on the nerve-forces within, followed by the same loss of muscular power, the same wide-awakeness of the reason, the same drawing out and concentrating of the energies on that spot in front, repeated itself—this time more deliberately, leaving me freer to take mental notes of what was happening. Again arose the noble, earnest figure, gazing at me, the hands moving in solemn accompaniment to the deep tones of voice. The same effort, painful on my part, to hear, with no result. The vision passed. Again the woman's face, insignificant and meaningless, succeeded it as before. She spoke, but in less emphatic tones. It flashed upon me that I *would* hear. After a frantic effort, I caught two words—'Land,' 'America'—with positively no clue to their meaning.

"I was wide awake when the first apparition appeared, and in a highly excited state of mind on its re-appearance."

HOW A GHOST WARNED THE KING

Kings and queens are not exempt from visitations of the supernatural; indeed, a large number of royal dignitaries have seen "ghosts," and have been haunted by specters in as unpleasant a manner as any ordinary mortal. Were we to hunt through the pages of history, we should find many of these—some of which it will doubtless be of interest to give at some future time. The following account is taken from the *Annals of the Kingdom of Scotland*, and is told in queer old English, with long 's's,' and so on, making it very hard to read in the original! I interpret it into modern English as best I can, maintaining its form:

"While James IV. stayed at Linlithgow, to gather up the scattered remains of his army, which had been defeated by the Earl of Surrey, at Flodden-field, he went into the Church of St. Michael there to hear evening prayer. While he was at his devotion, a remarkable figure of an ancient man, with flowing amber-colored hair hanging over his shoulders, his forehead high, and inclining to baldness, his garments of a fine blue color, somewhat long and girded together, with a fine white cloth, of comely and very reverent aspect, was seen inquiring for the king; when his majesty being pointed out to him he made his way through the crowd till he came to him, and then, with a clown's simplicity, leaning over the cannon's feet, he addressed him in the following words: 'Sir, I am sent hither to entreat you to delay your intended expedition for this time, and proceed no further; for if you do, you will be unfortunate, and not prosper in your enterprise, nor any of your followers. I am further charged to warn you, not to follow the acquaintance, company or counsel of women, as you value your life, honour and estate.'

"After giving him this admonition, he withdrew himself back through the crowd and disappeared.

"When service was ended, the king enquired earnestly after him, but he could not be found or heard of anywhere, neither could any of the bystanders (of whom many narrowly watched him, resolving afterwards to have discoursed with him) feel or perceive how, when or where he passed from them, having in a manner vanished from their sight.

"This caused the king to feel some uneasiness; 'for,' said he, 'if he were mortal man, how did he go so quickly hence, and how did he give me such advice, which I, of all men, know at this time to be of value?' The king was sorely puzzled; and called the warden of the church to him, and questioned him as to the man whom he had seen.

"And when the warden had heard the tale from the king, he questioned him in turn, as to the man's appearance—whether he was this and that; and of the man's manner of speech. And when the king had answered to his satisfaction, he turned pale; and said: 'Oh, king, the personage whom you saw to-day was not mortal man; but one dead long ago; one who lived and died close here; and known to many of us well. He has been known to come before in times of great stress; and his advice has always been good. Truly, my lord, you have this day seen an apparition of a dead man.'

"And the king marvelled at what he had seen."

Thus ends the curious old narrative. It will be seen that several others saw the ghost besides the king. These are called "collective cases" by those engaged in psychical studies; for the reason that several persons saw the figure at the same time, or "collectively." Such cases have never been satisfactorily explained. For, if the phantom were a mere hallucination, as many claim, how did several see it at once?

THE STAINS OF BLOOD

The following narrative was personally related to Robert Dale Owen, by a clergyman of the Church of England, who was Chaplain, at the time, to the British Legation in Florence. It is as follows:

"In the year 1856, I was staying with my wife and children, at a favorite watering place. In order to attend to some affairs of my own, I determined to leave my family there for three or four days. Accordingly, on the 8th of August, I took the railway, and arrived that evening an unexpected guest at the Hall—the residence of a gentleman whose acquaintance I had recently made, and with whom my sister was then staying.

"I arrived late, soon afterwards went to bed, and before long fell asleep. Awaking after three or four hours, I was not surprised to find that I could sleep no more—for I never rest well in a strange bed. After trying, therefore, in vain to induce sleep, I began to arrange my plans for the day. I had been engaged some little time in this way, when I became suddenly sensitive to the fact that there was a light in the room. Turning round, I distinctly perceived a female figure; and what attracted my special attention was that the light by which I saw it emanated from itself. I watched the figure attentively. The features were not perceptible. After moving a little distance, it disappeared as suddenly as it had appeared.

"My first thoughts were that there was some trick. I immediately got out of bed, struck a light, and found my bedroom door still locked. I then carefully examined the walls, to ascertain if there was any other concealed means of entrance or exit, but none could I find. I drew the curtains and opened the shutters, but all outside was silent and dark, there being no moonlight. After examining the room in every part, I went back to bed, and began thinking calmly over the whole matter. What had I seen? And why did *It appear*?

"In the morning, as soon as I was up and dressed, I told my sister what I had seen. She then informed me that the house had the reputation of being 'haunted'; and that a murder had been committed in it; but not in the room in which I had slept. Later in the day I left—after making my sister promise to do all she could to unravel the mystery.

"On the following Wednesday morning, I received a letter from my sister, in which she informed me that, since I left, she had made inquiries and had ascertained that the murder *was* committed in the very room in which I slept! She added that she proposed visiting us the next day, and that she would like me to write out an account of what I had seen—together with a plan of the room, and that on that plan she wished me to mark the place of the appearance and disappearance of the figure.

"This I immediately did; and the next day when my sister arrived, she asked me if I had complied with her request? I replied, pointing to the drawing room table: 'Yes, there is the account and the plan.'

"As she rose to examine it, I prevented her, saying:

'Do not look at it until you have told me all you have to say, because you might unintentionally color your story by what you may read there.'

"Thereupon she informed me that she had had the carpet taken up in the room I had occupied, and that the marks of blood from the murdered person were there, plainly visible, on a particular part of the floor. At my request she also then drew a plan of the room, and marked upon it the spots which still bore traces of blood. The two plans—my sister's and mine—were now compared; and we verified the most remarkable fact that *the place she had marked as the beginning and ending of the traces of blood coincided exactly with the spots marked on my plan as those on which the female figure had appeared and disappeared*!"

FACE TO FACE!

The following case is recorded by the wife of Colonel Lewin, and is reported in the *Proceedings* of the S. P. R.:

"In January, 1868, I took a house close to Hastings.... One night there was a heavy storm, the weather was bitterly cold, and a fire was burning in my bedroom when I went to bed at 10.30. I tried to go to sleep, but it was no use; the noise of the wind and the rain kept me awake. I must have been lying like this for a couple of hours when I became conscious of what seemed like a light in the room.... I thought the fire must have re-kindled itself, and crawled along on my knees on the bed to look at the fire over the high wooden foot, to see how this might be. I had no thought of anything but the fire, and was not nervous in the slightest degree. As I raised myself on my knees and looked over the foot of the bed, I found myself face to face, at a distance of about three feet, with the semblance of a man. I never for a moment thought he was a man, but was struck with the feeling that this was one from the dead.

"The light seemed to emanate from round this figure, but the only portions which I saw clearly were the head and shoulders. The face I shall never forget; it was pale, emaciated, with a thin, high-bridged nose, and eyes deeply sunk and glowing in the sockets with a sort of glare. A long beard was seemingly rolled in under a white comforter, and on the head was a slouched felt hat. I had a nervous shock, and felt a dead person was looking upon *me*—a living one, but had no sensation of being actually frightened, until the figure moved slowly as if interposing between me and the door, then horror overcame me and I fell back in a dead faint. How long I remained unconscious I know not, but I came to myself cold and cramped; the room was quite dark and nothing was visible. Thoroughly tired out, I got into bed, and slept soundly until morning."

JULIA, DARLING!

The next example is from the *Proceedings* of the S. P. R. (Vol. V., pp. 440-41), and Mr. Myers states that the writer was well known to him. The account reads in part:

"My mother died on the 24th of June, 1874, at Slima, Malta, where we were then residing for her health. Seven nights later she appeared to me.... I seemed to have been sleeping some time when I woke, and, turning over on the other side towards the window, saw my mother standing by my bedside, crying and wringing her hands. I had not been awake long enough to remember that she was dead, and exclaimed quite naturally, 'Why, dear, what's the matter?' and then suddenly remembering, I screamed. The nurse sprang up from the next room, but on the top step flung herself on her knees and began to tell her beads and cry. My father at the same moment arrived at the opposite door, and I heard his sudden exclamation of 'Julia, darling.' My mother turned towards him, and then to me, and, wringing her hands again, retreated towards the nursery and was lost. The nurse afterwards stated that she distinctly felt something pass her.... My father ordered her out of the room, and telling me that I had only been dreaming, stayed until I fell asleep. The next day, however, he told me that he, too, had seen the vision, and that he hoped to do so again, and that if ever she came to see me ... I was not to be frightened ... but she never appeared again."

THE CUT ACROSS THE CHEEK

In the narrative which follows, the apparition conveyed—by its very appearance—information which the percipient could not possibly have known. It is from Mr. H. Walton, of Dent, Sedburgh, England, and was sent to Mr. Stead, who published it:

"In the month of April, 1881, I was located in Norfolk, and my duties took me once a fortnight to a fishing village on the coast—so I can guarantee the following facts: It is customary for the fishing smacks to go to Grimsby 'line fishing' in the spring. The vessels started one afternoon on their journey north. In the evening, a heavy north-east wind blew, and one of the boats mistook the white surf on the rocks for the reflection of a lighthouse. In consequence the boat got into shallow water, a heavy sea came, and swept two men from the deck. One man grasped a rope and was saved; the other, a younger man, failed to save himself, though an expert swimmer. It was said that he was heard to shout about 11 o'clock.

"Towards one o'clock, the young man's mother, lying awake, saw his apparition come to the foot of the bed, clad in white, and she screamed with fright, and told her husband what she had seen, and that J. was drowned. He sought in vain to calm her by saying that she must have been dreaming. She asserted the contrary. Next day, when her daughter came in with the telegram of the sad event, before her daughter had time to speak, she cried out: 'J. is drowned,' and became unconscious; she remained in this state for many hours. When she regained consciousness, she told them particularly and distinctly what she had seen; and what is to the point is this remarkable thing: she said: 'If ever the body is found, it has a cut across the cheek,'—specifying which cheek. The body was found some days after, and exactly as mother had seen it, was the cut on the cheek."

THE INVISIBLE HAND

The following account was sent to the S. P. R. Ghosts are usually *seen*; they are sometimes heard; they are very rarely *felt*. The account which follows is an example of the latter class, in which the ghost was not only seen but touched.

After stating that she was visiting a friend of hers in the country, when the event occurred, the narrator proceeds:

"We went upstairs together, I being perhaps a couple of steps behind my friend, when, on reaching the topmost step, I felt something suddenly slip behind me from an unoccupied room on the left of the stairs. Thinking it must be imagination, no one being in the house except the widow and servant, who occupied rooms on another landing, I did not speak to my friend, who turned off to a room on the right, but walked quickly into my room, which faced the staircase, still feeling as though a tall figure was bending over me. I turned on the gas, struck a light, and was in the act of applying it, when I felt a heavy grasp on my arm of a hand, minus the middle finger. Upon this I uttered a loud cry, which brought my friend, the widow lady, and the servant girl, into the room to inquire the cause of my alarm. The two latter turned very pale on hearing the story. The house was thoroughly searched, but nothing was discovered.

"Some weeks passed, and I had ceased to be alarmed at the occurrence, when I chanced to mention it whilst spending the afternoon with some friends. A gentleman asked me if I had ever heard a description or seen a 'carte' of the lady's late husband. On receiving a reply in the negative, he said, singularly enough, he was tall, had a slight stoop, and has lost the middle finger on his hand! On my return, I inquired of the servant, who had been in the family from childhood, if such were the case, and learned that it was quite correct, and that she (the girl) had once, when sleeping in the same room, awakened on feeling some one pressing down her knees, and on opening her eyes saw her late master by the bed side—on which she fainted, and had never dared to enter the room after dark since. She is not an imaginative girl; nor am I. When I was grasped, however, *I* did not *see* anything.

"But worse was to follow! It so chanced that I had to sleep in that room once again, as the house was full of company, and there was nowhere else for me to go. I had by this time got over my fears, and hardly minded the idea of sleeping in the room at all. I left the room door open, turned out the light and was soon sound asleep.

"Some time in the early hours of the morning I awoke with an indescribable feeling. I was *suddenly* wide awake—without the slightest traces of sleep; yet I did not know *how* I awoke; and had not any recollection of waking. But there I was wide awake, and staring up at the ceiling with wide-open eyes. My right hand was hanging over the side of the bed; so that it fell outwards, into the room. Imagine my horror, then, in feeling a hand suddenly grasp my hand, and I felt distinctly that it was *minus the middle finger*. The hand was icy cold, and of a peculiar hardness. I hung on to the hand, however, determined to go to the bottom of the affair. I gripped tightly; and still retained the hand in my grip. Bending over, I stretched out my left hand, and, with the fingers of that hand, felt over the hand and wrist I was holding. I then commenced to trace it up the arm. I had about reached the elbow—or a little below—when the arm suddenly ended—came to nothing; was no more! Yet the hand in mine was as solid as ever. This gave me such a shock that I let go the hand I was holding, and sank back onto my pillows. Then terror took possession of me; and I do not know what happened later. I only know that I had brain fever, which laid me low for several weeks. The occurrence has never been explained."

THE APPARITION OF THE RADIANT BOY

The following is a famous case, well-known as the "Apparition of the Radiant Boy." It was seen by the Marquis of Londonderry, and frequently spoken of by him afterwards.

At the time of the appearance, Lord Londonderry was on a visit to a friend in the North of Ireland. The apartment assigned to him was one calculated to foster the belief in ghosts, because of its richly carved paneling—its huge fireplace, looking like the open entrance into a tomb—and the vast, ponderous draperies that hung in thick folds around the room.

Lord Londonderry examined his chamber; he made himself acquainted with the forms and faces of the ancient possessors of the mansion, whose portraits hung around the room. Then, after dismissing his valet, he retired to bed.

His candles had not long been extinguished when he perceived a light gleaming on the draperies of the lofty canopies over his head. Conscious that there was no fire in the grate—that the curtains were closed—that the chamber had been in perfect darkness but a few minutes before, he supposed that some intruder must have accidentally entered his apartment; and, turning hastily around to the side from which the light proceeded, saw, to his infinite astonishment, not the form of a human visitor, but the figure of a fair boy, who seemed to be garmented in rays of mild and tempered glory, which beamed palely from his slender form, like the faint light of the declining moon and rendered the objects nearest to him dimly and indistinctly visible. The spirit stood but a short distance from the side of the bed.

Certain that his own faculties were not deceiving him, Lord Londonderry got up and moved towards the figure. It retreated before him; as he slowly advanced, and with equal pace, slowly retired. It entered the gloomy arch of the capacious chimney, and then sank into the earth. Lord Londonderry returned to his bed, but not to rest; his mind was harassed by the consideration of the extraordinary event which had occurred to him. Was it real? Was it the work of imagination? Was it the result of imposture? It was all incomprehensible.

He resolved in the morning not to mention the appearance till he should have well observed the manners and countenances of the family; he was conscious that, if any deception had been practised, its authors would be too delighted with their success to conceal the vanity of their triumph.

When the guests assembled at the breakfast table, the eye of Lord Londonderry searched in vain for latent smiles—those conscious looks—that silent communication between the parties, by which the authors of such domestic conspiracies are generally betrayed. Everything, apparently, proceeded in its ordinary course. At last the hero of the tale felt bound to mention the occurrence of the night.

At its conclusion, his host said: "The circumstances which you have just recounted appear very extraordinary to those who have not long been inmates of my dwelling; and are not conversant with the legends of my family; and to those who are, the event which has happened will only serve as the corroboration of an old tradition that has long been related of the apartment in which you slept. You have seen the 'Radiant Boy'; be content—it is an omen of prosperous fortunes. I would rather that this subject should not be mentioned." And here the affair ended.

FISHER'S GHOST

The following incident comes from Australia, and is well-known in that part of the world. It is usually known as "Fisher's Ghost," and is to the following effect:

"A number of years ago, a free settler, named John Fisher, who had long successfully cultivated a grant of land in a remote district, and who was known to be possessed of a considerable sum of money, had been missing for some time after having visited the nearest market town, whither he had been in the habit of repairing with cattle and produce for sale.

"An inquiry was instituted by his acquaintances; but his head servant, or rather his assistant on the farm—an ex-convict, who had lived many years with him in that situation—declared that his master had left the colony for some time on business, and that he expected him to return in a few months. As this man was generally known as Fisher's confidential servant, his assertion was believed—though some expressed surprise at the settler's abrupt and clandestine departure; for his character was good in every way. The 'month's wonder' soon subsided, however, and Fisher was forgotten. His assistant, meanwhile, managed the farm, bought and sold, and spent money freely. If questioned, which was but rarely, he would express his surprise at his master's delay, and pretend to expect him daily.

"A few months after he had been first missed, a neighbouring settler, who was returning late on Saturday night from the market town, had occasion to pass within half a mile of Fisher's house. As he was riding by the fence which separated the farm from the high road, he distinctly saw the figure of a man seated on the railing, and at once recognized the form and features of his lost neighbor.

"He instantly stopped and called to him by name; but the figure descended from the railing, and pointing appealingly toward the house, walked slowly across the field in that direction. The settler, having lost sight of him in the gloom, proceeded on his journey, and informed his family and neighbors that he had seen Fisher and spoken to him. On inquiry, however, Fisher's assistant said that he had not arrived, and affected to laugh at the settler's story—insinuating that he had probably drunk too freely at the market.

"The neighbors were, however, not satisfied. The strange appearance of Fisher, sitting on the rail and pointing, with so much meaning, toward his own house aroused their suspicions, and they insisted upon a strict and immediate investigation by the police.

"The party of investigators took with them an old and clever native. They had not proceeded far in the underbrush when they discovered a log, on which was a dark brown stain. This the native examined, and at once declared it to be '*white man's blood*.' He then, without hesitation, set off at a full run, toward a pond not far from the house.

"He ran backwards and forwards about the pond, like a dog on the scent; and finally, borrowing a ramrod from one of the settlers, ran it into the earth. He did this in one or two places; and finally said: '*White man here.*'

"The spot was immediately dug up, and a corpse, identified as that of Fisher, was discovered, its skull fractured, and evidently many weeks buried.

"The guilty assistant was immediately arrested, and tried at Sydney, on circumstantial evidence alone—strong enough, however, to convict him, in spite of his self-possession, and protestations of innocence. He was sentenced to death; and, previous to his execution, made an ample confession of his guilt."

HARRIET HOSMER'S VISION

Lydia Maria Child relates the following interesting narrative:

"When Harriet Hosmer, the sculptor, visited her native country a few years ago, I had an interview with her, during which our conversation happened to turn on dreams and visions.

"'I have had some experience in that way,' said she. 'Let me tell you a singular circumstance that happened to me in Rome. An Italian girl named Rosa was in my employ for a long time, but was finally obliged to return to her mother on account of confirmed ill-health. We were mutually sorry to part, for we liked each other. When I took my customary exercise on horseback, I frequently called to see her. On one of these occasions, I found her brighter than I had seen her for some time past. I had long relinquished hopes of her recovery, but there was nothing in her appearance that gave the appearance of immediate danger. I left her with the expectation of calling to see her again many times. During the remainder of the day, I was busy in my studio, and I do not recollect that Rosa was in my thoughts after I had parted from her. I retired to rest in good health, and in a quiet frame of mind. But I woke from a sound sleep with the oppressive feeling that someone was in the room. I wondered at the sensation, for it was entirely new to me; but in vain I tried to dispel it. I peered beyond the curtains of my bed but could distinguish no objects in the darkness. Trying to gather my thoughts I reflected that the door was locked, and that I had put the key under my bolster. I felt for it and found it where I had placed it. I said to myself that I had probably had some ugly dream, and had waked with a vague impression of it still on my mind. Reasoning thus, I arranged myself comfortably for another nap.

"'I am habitually a good sleeper and a stranger to fear, but do what I would, the idea still haunted me that someone was in the room. Finding it impossible to sleep, I longed for daylight to dawn, that I might rise and pursue my customary avocation. It was not long before I was able dimly to distinguish the furniture in my room, and, soon after, to hear familiar noises of servants opening windows and doors. An old clock with ringing vibration, proclaimed the hour. I counted one, two, three, four, five, and resolved to rise immediately. My bed was partially screened by a long curtain looped up at one side. As I raised my head from the pillow, Rosa looked inside the curtain, and smiled at me. The idea of anything supernatural did not occur to me. I was simply surprised and exclaimed: "Why, Rosa! How came you here when you are so ill?"

"'In the old familiar tone to which I was so much accustomed, a voice replied, "I am well now."

"'With no other thought but that of greeting her joyfully, I sprang out of bed. There was no Rosa there! When I became convinced that there was no one in the room but myself, I recollected the fact that my door was locked, and thought I must have seen a vision.

"'At the breakfast table, I said to the old lady with whom I boarded: "Rosa is dead." I then summoned a messenger and sent him to inquire how Rosa was. He returned with the answer that she died that morning at 5 o'clock.'

"I wrote the story as Miss Hosmer told it to me, and after I had shown it to her, I asked her if she had any objection to its being published without suppression of names. She replied: 'You have reported the story of Rosa correctly. Make what use you please of it. You cannot think it more interesting or unaccountable than I do myself.'"

THE APPARITION OF THE MURDERED BOY

At the commencement of the French Revolution, Lady Pennyman and her two daughters and her friend, Mrs. Atkins, retired to Lisle, where they had hired a large and handsome house. A few weeks after taking possession, the housekeeper, with many apologies for being obliged to mention anything that might appear so idle and absurd, came to the apartment in which her mistress was sitting, and said that two of the servants who had accompanied her ladyship from England had that morning given warning, and expressed a determination of quitting her ladyship's service, on account of the mysterious noises by which they had been night after night disturbed and terrified. The room from which the sounds were supposed to have proceeded was at a distance from Lady Pennyman's apartments, and immediately over those that were occupied by the servants. To quiet the alarm Lady Pennyman resolved on leaving her own chamber for a time and establishing herself in the one which had been lately occupied by the domestics.

The room above was a long, spacious one, which appeared to have been for a long time deserted. In the center of the chamber was a large iron cage. It was said that the late proprietor of the house—a young man of enormous wealth—had in his minority been confined in this cage by his uncle and guardian and starved to death.

On the first night or two of Lady Pennyman's being established in her new apartment, she met with no interruption. This quiet, however, was of very short duration. One night she was awakened from her sleep by a slow and heavy step pacing the chamber overhead. It continued to move backwards and forwards for nearly an hour. There were more complaints from the housekeeper, no servants would remain. Lady

Pennyman began herself to be alarmed. She requested the advice of Mrs. Atkins—a woman devoid of every kind of superstitious fear, and of tried courage. Mrs. Atkins determined to make the Cage room itself her sleeping quarters. A bed was accordingly placed in the apartment, and Mrs. Atkins retired to rest attended by her favorite spaniel—saying, as she bade them all good-night, "I and my dog are able to compete with a myriad of ghosts."

Mrs. Atkins examined the chamber in every imaginable direction; she sounded every panel of the wainscot to prove there was no hollowness that might argue a concealed passage; and having securely bolted the door of the room, retired to rest, confident that she was secure against every material visitor, and totally incredulous of the airy encroachments of spiritual beings. She had only been asleep a few minutes, when her dog, which lay by her bedside, leaped, howling and terrified, on the bed. The bolted door of the chamber slowly opened and a pale, thin, sickly youth came in, cast his eyes mildly toward her, walked up to the iron cage in the middle of the room, and then leaned in the melancholy attitude of one revolving in his mind the sorrows of a cheerless and unblest existence. After a while he again withdrew, and retired by the way he entered.

Mrs. Atkins, on witnessing his departure, felt the return of her resolution. She persuaded herself to believe the figure the work of some skillful imposter, and she determined on following its footsteps. She took up her lamp and hastened to the door. To her infinite surprise, she discovered it to be fastened, as she had herself left it on retiring to bed. On withdrawing the bolt, and opening the door, she saw the back of the youth descending the staircase. She followed till, on reaching the foot of the stairs, the form seemed to sink into the earth.

The event was related to Lady Pennyman. She determined to remain no longer in her present habitation. Another residence was offered in the vicinity of Lisle, and this she took under the pretext that it was better suited to the size of her family.

THE GHOST IN YELLOW CALICO

The Rev. Elwyn Thomas, 35, Park Village East, N. W., London, has published a very remarkable experience of his own. It is as follows:

"Twelve years ago," says the doctor, "I was the second minister of the Bryn Mawr Welsh Wesleyan Circuit, in the South Wales District. It was a beautiful evening in June when, after conducting the service at Llanyndir, I told the gentlemen with whom I generally stayed when preaching there, that three young friends had come to meet me from Crickhowell, and that I meant to accompany them back for about half a mile on their return journey, so would not be home before nine o'clock.

"When I wished good-night to my friends it was about twenty minutes to nine but still light enough to see a good distance. The subject of our conversation all the way from the chapel until we parted was of a certain eccentric old character who then belonged to the Crickhowell church. I walked a little further down the road than I intended in order to hear the end of a very amusing story about him. Our conversation had no reference whatever to ghosts. Personally I was a strong disbeliever in ghosts and invariably ridiculed anyone whom I thought superstitious enough to believe in them.

"When I had walked about a hundred yards away from my friends, after parting from them, I saw on the bank of the canal, what I thought at the moment was an old beggar. I couldn't help asking myself where this old man had come from. I had not seen him in going down the road. I turned round quite unconcernedly to have another look at him, and had no sooner done so than I saw, within half a yard of me one of the most remarkable and startling sights I hope it will ever be my lot to see. Almost on a level with my own face, I saw that of an old man, over every feature of which the putty colored skin was drawn tightly, except the forehead which was lined with deep wrinkles. The lips were extremely thin and appeared perfectly bloodless. The toothless mouth stood half open. The cheeks were hollow and sunken like those of a corpse, and the eyes which seemed far back in the middle of the head, were unnaturally luminous and piercing. The terrible object was wrapped in two bands of old yellow calico, one of which was drawn under the chin, and over the cheeks and tied at the top of the head, the other was drawn round the top of the wrinkled forehead and fastened at the back of the head. So deep and indelible an impression it made on my mind, that, were I an artist, I could paint that face to-day.

"What I have thus tried to describe in many words, I saw at a glance. Acting on the impulse of the moment, I turned my face toward the village and ran away from the horrible vision with all my might for about sixty yards. I then stopped and turned around to see how far I had distanced it, and to my unspeakable horror, there it was still face to face with me as if I had not moved an inch. I grasped my umbrella and raised it to strike him, and you can imagine my feelings when I could see nothing between the face and the ground, except an irregular column of intense darkness, through which my umbrella passed as a stick goes through water!

"I am sorry to say that I took to my heels with increasing speed. A little further than the space of this second encounter, the road which led to my host's house branched off the main road. Having gone two or three yards down this branch road, I turned around again. He had not followed me after I left the main road, but I could see the horribly fascinating face quite as plainly as when it was close by. It stood for a few minutes looking intently at me from the center of the main road. I then realized fully that it was not a human being in flesh and blood; and, with every vestige of fear gone, I quickly walked toward it to put my questions. But I was disappointed, for, no sooner had I made toward it, than it began to move slowly down the road keeping the same distance above it until it reached the churchyard wall; it then crossed the road and disappeared near where the yew tree stood inside. The moment it disappeared, I became unconscious. Two hours later I came to myself and I made my way slowly to my home. I could not say a word to explain what had happened, though I tried several times. It was five o'clock in the morning when I regained my power of speech. The whole of the following week I was laid up with a nervous prostration.

"My host, after questioning me closely, told me that fifteen years before that time an old recluse of eccentric character, answering in every detail to my description (yellow calicoes, bands, and all) lived in a house whose ruins still stand close by where I saw the face disappear."

CHAPTER III

MORE PHANTASMS OF THE DEAD—II.

THE cases included in this chapter are also very well authenticated—some of them being longer and more detailed than those included in the last chapter. I shall begin with a group of so-called "Pact" Cases—cases, that is, in which a Pact or Agreement was made before death—to appear after death, if possible; when that promise seems to have been kept. The first case of this character is short, and merely illustrative of the kind of ghostly phenomena to be expected in cases of this nature. The latter cases are better attested. I give first the case of the Marquis of Rambouillet.

COMPACTS TO APPEAR AFTER DEATH

The story of the Marquis of Rambouillet's appearing after his death to his cousin, the Marquis de Precy, is well authenticated. These two noblemen, talking one day concerning the affairs of the next world, in a manner which showed they did not believe much about it, entered into an agreement that the first who died should come and give intelligence to the other.

Soon afterwards the Marquis of Rambouillet set out for Flanders, which was then the seat of war, and the Marquis de Precy remained in Paris, being ill of a violent fever. About six weeks after, early one morning, he heard someone draw the curtains of his bed, and turning to see who it was, discovered the Marquis of Rambouillet in a buff coat and boots. He instantly got out of bed, and attempted to shake hands with his friend, but Rambouillet drew back, and told him he had only come to perform the promise he had formerly made; that nothing was more certain than another life; and that he earnestly advised him to alter his mode of life, for in the first battle he would be engaged in, he would certainly fall.

Precy made a fresh attempt to touch his friend, but he immediately withdrew. Precy lay upon his bed wondering upon the strangeness of the circumstances for some time, when he saw the same appearance re-enter the apartment. Rambouillet, finding that Precy still disbelieved what he was told, showed him the wound of which he had died, and from which the blood still seemed to flow.

Soon after this, Precy received a confirmation of Rambouillet's death, and was killed himself, according to the prediction, in the civil wars, at the battle of Faubourg St. Antoine.

— HEREWARD CARRINGTON —

LORD BROUGHAM'S VISION

The promise to appear was given and kept in the case of the apparition seen by Lord Brougham.

The story is given as follows in the first volume of "Lord Brougham's Memoirs":

"A most remarkable thing happened to me, so remarkable that I must tell the story from the beginning. After I left the High School I went with G——, my most intimate friend, to attend the classes in the University. There was no divinity class, but we frequently in our walks discussed many grave subjects—among others the immortality of the soul and a future state. This question, and the possibility of the dead appearing to the living, were the subject of much speculation, and we actually committed the folly of drawing up an agreement, written with our blood, to the effect that whichever of us died the first should appear to the other, and thus solve any doubts we had entertained of the 'life after death.' After we had finished our classes at the College, G—— went to India, having got an appointment there in the Civil Service. He seldom wrote to me, and after a lapse of a few years I had nearly forgotten his existence.... One day I had taken, as I have said, a warm bath, and, while lying in it and enjoying the comfort of the heat, I turned my head round, looking towards the chair on which I had deposited my clothes, as I was about to get out of the bath. On the chair sat G——, looking calmly at me! How I got out of the bath I know not; but on recovering my senses, I found myself sprawling on the floor.

The apparition, or whatever it was that had taken the likeness of G——, had disappeared. This vision had produced such a shock that I had no inclination to talk about it, or to speak about it even to Stewart, but the impression it made upon me was too vivid to be easily forgotten, and so strongly was I affected by it that I have here written down the whole history, with the date, December 19th, and all the particulars, as they are now fresh before me. No doubt I had fallen asleep, and that the apparition presented so distinctly before my eyes was a dream I cannot for a moment doubt; yet for years I had had no communication with G——, nor had there been anything to recall him to my recollection. Nothing had taken place concerning our Swedish travels connected with G——, or with India, or with anything relating to him, or to any member of his family. I recollected quickly enough our old discussion, and the bargain we had made. I could not discharge from my mind the impression that G—— must have died, and that his appearance to me was to be received by me as a proof of a future state. This was on December 19th, 1799."

In October, 1862, Lord Brougham added as a Postscript:

"I have just been copying out from my Journal the account of this strange dream. *Certissima mortis imago*! And now to finish the story begun about sixty years ago: Soon after my return to Edinborough there arrived a letter from India announcing G——'s death, and stating that he died on December 19th."

Lord Brougham attempts to account for this vision by stating that it was probably a dream. But this is negatived by the fact that he was so startled by it as to scramble out of the bath in a great hurry—which would not be at all likely had it been a dream—for, as we know, nothing surprises us in dreams, or seems unlikely. And even granting that it were a dream, we still have the *coincidence* to account for. *Why* should Lord Brougham have dreamed this particular dream at the very moment his friend died? That fact has yet to be accounted for.

THE TYRONE GHOST

This is also known as the Beresford Ghost, and is one of the most famous cases of its kind on record. The account, as herein given, is that supplied by the granddaughter of Lady Beresford, to whom the experience came; and hence may be considered as accurate as it can be made. It furnishes us with a definite example of a "ghost that touches," and leaves a permanent mark of its visit, ever afterwards. Here is the account:

"In the month of October, 1693, Sir Tristram and Lady Beresford went on a visit to her sister, Lady Macgill, at Gill Hall, now the seat of Lord Clanwilliam.... One morning Sir Tristram arose early, leaving Lady Beresford asleep, and went out for a walk before breakfast. When his wife joined the table very late, her appearance and the embarrassment of her manner attracted general attention, especially that of her husband. He made anxious inquiries as to her health, and asked her apart what had happened to her wrist, which was tied up with black ribbon tightly bound round it. She earnestly entreated him not to inquire more then, or thereafter, as to the cause of her wearing or continuing afterwards to wear that ribbon; 'for,' she added, 'you will never see me without it.' He replied: 'Since you urge it so vehemently, I promise you not to inquire more about it.'

"After completing her hurried breakfast, she made inquiries as to whether the post had yet arrived. It had not yet come in, and Sir Tristram asked: 'Why are you so particularly eager about letters to-day?' 'Because I expect to hear of Lord Tyrone's death, which took place on Tuesday.' 'Well,' remarked Sir Tristram, 'I never put you down for a superstitious person, but I suppose that some idle dream has disturbed you.' Shortly after, the servant brought in the letters; one was sealed with black wax. 'It is as I expected,' she cried, 'he is dead.' The letter was from Lord Tyrone's steward to inform them that his master had died in Dublin, on Tuesday, 14 October, at 4 p.m. Sir Tristram endeavored to console her, and begged her to restrain her grief, when she assured him that she felt relieved and easier, now that she knew the actual fact. She added, 'I can now give you a most satisfactory piece of intelligence, *viz.*, that I am with child, and that it will be a boy.' A son was born the following July.

"On her forty-seventh birthday, Lady Beresford summoned her children to her side, and said to them: 'I have something of deep importance to communicate to you, my dear children, before I die. You are no strangers to the intimacy and affection which subsisted in early life between Lord Tyrone and myself.... We had made a solemn promise to one another, that whichever died first should, if permitted, appear to the other.... One night, years after this interchange of promises, I was sleeping with your father at Gill Hall, when I suddenly awoke and discovered Lord Tyrone sitting visibly by the side of the bed. I screamed out and vainly tried to arouse Sir Tristram. "Tell me," I said, "Lord Tyrone, why and wherefore are you here at this time of the night?" "Have you then forgotten our promises to each other, pledged in early life? I died on Tuesday, at 4 o'clock. I have been permitted thus to appear.... I am also suffered to inform you that you are with child, and will produce a son, who will marry an heiress; that Sir Tristram will not live long, that you will marry again, and you will die in your forty-seventh year." I begged from him some convincing sign or proof so that when the morning came I might rely upon it, and that it was not the phantom of my imagination. He caused the hangings of the bed to be drawn in an unusual way and impossible manner through an iron hook. I still was not satisfied, when he wrote his signature in my pocketbook. I wanted, however, more substantial proof of his visit, when he laid his hand, which was cold as marble, on my wrist; the sinews shrunk up, the nerves withered at the touch. "Now," he said, "let no mortal eye while you live ever see that wrist," and vanished. While I was conversing with him my thoughts were calm, but as soon as he disappeared I felt chilled with horror and dismay, a cold sweat came over me, and I again endeavored, but vainly, to awaken Sir Tristram; a flood of tears came to my relief, and I fell asleep....'

"That year Lady Beresford died. On her deathbed, Lady Riverson unbound the black ribbon and found the wrist exactly as Lady Beresford had described it—every nerve withered, every sinew shrunk...."

"DEAD OR ALIVE"

In the following case the ghost kept its promise to appear—doing so, to all appearances, in spite of great obstacles. The incident is reported in Mr. W. T. Stead's *Real Ghost Stories*, pp. 205-8:

"The following incident occurred to me some years ago, and all the details can be substantiated. The date was August 26, 1867, at midnight. I was then residing in the neighborhood of Hull, and held an appointment under the crown which necessitated my repairing thither every day for a few hours duty. My berth was almost a sinecure; and I had for some time been engaged to a young north country heiress, it being understood that on our marriage I should take her name and 'stand for the county' or rather for one of its divisions.

"For her sake I had to break off a love affair, not of the most reputable order, with a girl in Hull. I will call her Louise. She was young, beautiful, and devoted to me. On the night of the 26th of August we took our last walk together, and a few minutes before midnight paused on a wooden bridge running across a kind of canal, locally termed a 'drain.' We paused on the bridge, listening to the swirling of the current against the wooden piles, and waiting for the stroke of midnight to part forever. In the few minutes interval she repeated *sotto voce*, Longfellow's 'Bridge,' the words of which, 'I stood on the bridge at midnight,' seemed terribly appropriate. After nearly twenty-five years I can never hear that piece recited without feeling a deadly chill, and the whole scene of two souls in agony again rising before me. Well! Midnight struck and we parted; but Louise said: 'Grant me one favor, the only one that I shall ever ask you on this earth; promise to meet me here twelve months from to-night at this same hour.' I demurred at first, thinking it would be bad for both of us, and only re-open partially-healed wounds. At last, however, I consented, saying, 'Well, I will come if I am alive.' But she said, 'Say alive or dead.' I said, 'Very well, then, we will meet, dead or alive.'

"The next year I was on the spot a few minutes before the time; and, punctual to the stroke of midnight, Louise arrived. By this time I had begun to regret the arrangement I had made; but it was of too solemn a nature to put aside. I therefore kept the appointment; but said that I did not care to renew the compact. Louise, however, persuaded me to renew it for one more year; and I consented, much against my will; and we again left each other, repeating the same formula, 'Dead or Alive.'

"The next year after passed rapidly until the first week in July, when I was shot dangerously in the thigh by a fisherman named Thomas Piles, of Hull, a reputed smuggler. A party of four of us had hired his ten-ton yawl to go yachting round the Yorkshire coast, and amuse ourselves by shooting sea-birds amongst the millions of them at Flamborough Head. The third or fourth day out I was shot in the right thigh by the skipper Piles; and the day after, one and a quarter ounce of number 2 shot were cut out therefrom by the coastguard surgeon at Bridlington Quay (whose name I forget for the moment), assisted by Dr. Alexander Mackey, at the Black Lion hotel. The affair was in all the papers at the time, about a column of it appearing in the *Eastern Morning News*, of Hull.

"As soon as I was able to be removed (two or three weeks) I was taken home, where Dr. Melburne King, of Hull, attended me. The day—and the night—(the 26th of August) came. I was then unable to walk without crutches, and that for only a short distance, so had to be wheeled about in a Bath chair. The distance to the trysting place being rather long, and the time and the circumstances being very peculiar, I did not avail myself of the services of my usual attendant, but specially retained an old servant of the family, who frequently did confidential commissions for me, and who knew Miss Louise well. We set forth 'without beat of drum' and arrived at the bridge about a few minutes to midnight. I remember that it was a brilliant starlight night, but I do not think that there was any moon—at all events, at that hour. 'Old Bob,' as he was always affectionately called, wheeled me to the bridge, helped me out of the Bath chair, and gave me my crutch. I walked on to the bridge, and leaned my back against the white painted rail top, then lighted my briar-root, and had a comfortable smoke.

"I was very much annoyed that I had allowed myself to be persuaded to come a second time, and determined to tell Louise positively that this should be our last meeting. Besides, *now*, I did not consider it fair to Miss K., with whom I was again 'negotiating.' So, if anything, it was in rather a sulky frame of mind that I awaited Louise. Just as the quarters before the hour began to chime I distinctly heard the 'clink, clink' of the little brass heels, which she always wore, sounding on the long flagged causeway, leading for 200 yards up to the bridge. As she got nearer, I could see her pass lamp after lamp in rapid succession, while the strokes of the large clock at Hull resounded through the stilly night.

"At last the patter, patter of the tiny feet sounded on the woodwork of the bridge, and I saw her distinctly pass under the lamp at my side. When she got close to me I saw that she had neither hat nor cape on, and concluded that she had taken a cab at the further end of the flagged causeway, and (it being a very warm night) had left her wraps in the cab, and, for purposes of effect, had come the short distance in evening dress.

"'Clink, clink,' went the brass heels, and she seemed about passing me, when I suddenly, urged by an impulse of affection, stretched out my arms to receive her. She passed *through* them, intangible, impalpable, and as she looked at me I distinctly saw her lips move, and form the words 'Dead or Alive.'

I even heard the words, but not with my outward ears, with something else, some other sense—what, I know not. I felt startled, surprised, but not afraid, until a moment afterwards, when I *felt*, but could not see, some other presence following her. I could *feel*, though I could not *hear*, the heavy, clumsy thud of feet following her; and my blood seemed turned to ice. Recovering myself with an effort, I shouted out to Old Bob, who was safely ensconsed with the Bath chair in a nook out of sight round the corner: 'Bob, who passed you just now?' In an instant the old Yorkshire-man was by my side. 'Ne'er a one passed me, sir.' 'Nonsense, Bob,' I replied, 'I told you that I was coming to meet Miss Louise, and she just passed me on the bridge, and *must* have passed you, because there is no where else she *could* go. You don't mean to tell me you didn't see her?' The old man replied solemnly: 'Maister Rob, there's something uncanny about it. I heered her come on the bridge, and off it, and I knaw them clickety heels onywhere! but I'm domned, sir, if she passed me! I'm thinking we'd better gang.' And 'gang' we did; and it was the small hours of the morning (getting daylight) before we left off talking over the affair, and went to bed.

"The next day I made inquiries from Louise's family about her, and ascertained that she had died in Liverpool three months previously, being apparently delirious for a few hours before her death, and, our parting compact evidently weighing on her mind, as she kept repeating, 'Dead or Alive—shall I be there?'—to the utter bewilderment of her friends, who could not divine her meaning—being, of course, entirely unaware of our agreement."

This completes the examples of the so-called "Pact" cases. In the following example, the phantasmal form conveyed a piece of information to the percipient which he could not well have known by any normal means.

THE SCRATCH ON THE CHEEK

The case appeared in the *Proceedings* of the Amer. S. P. R., and the high character of the witnesses was vouched for by Dr. Hodgson and Prof. Royce. It is to the following effect:

"January 11, 1888.
"Sir: Replying to your recently published request for actual occurrences of psychical phenomena, I respectively submit the following remarkable occurrence to the consideration of your distinguished Society, with the assurance that the event made a more powerful impression upon my mind than the combined incidents of my whole life.... I was never in better health or possessed a clearer head and mind than at the time the incident occurred.

"In 1867, my only sister, a young lady of eighteen years, died suddenly of cholera, in St. Louis, Mo. My attachment for her was very strong, and the blow a severe one to me. A year or so after her death, I became a commercial traveller, and it was in 1876, while on one of my Western trips that the event occurred.

"I had 'drummed' the city of St. Joseph, Mo., and had gone to my room at the Pacific House to send in my orders, which were unusually large ones, so that I was in a very happy frame of mind indeed. My thoughts, of course, were about these orders, knowing how pleased my house would be at my success. I had not been thinking of my late sister, or in any manner reflecting on the past. The hour was high noon, and the sun was shining cheerfully into my room. While busy smoking a cigar, and writing out my orders, I suddenly became conscious that some one was sitting on my left, with one arm resting on the table. Quick as a flash I turned, and distinctly saw the form of my dead sister, and for a brief second or two looked her squarely in the face; and so sure was I that it was she, that I sprang forward in delight, calling her by name, and, as I did so, the apparition instantly vanished. Naturally I was startled and dumbfounded, almost doubting my senses; but the cigar in my mouth, and pen in hand, with the ink still moist on my letter, I satisfied myself I had not been dreaming and was still awake. I was near enough to touch her, had it been a physical possibility, and noted her features, expression, and details of dress, etc. She appeared as if alive. Her eyes looked kindly and perfectly naturally into mine. Her skin was so perfectly life-like that I could see the glow or moisture in the surface, and, on the whole there was no change in her appearance, otherwise than when alive.

"Now comes the most remarkable confirmation of my statement, which cannot be doubted by those who know what I state actually occurred. This visitation, or whatever you may call it, so impressed me that I took the next train home, and in the presence of my parents and others I related what had occurred. My father, a man of rare good sense and very practical, was inclined to ridicule me, as he saw how earnestly I believed what I stated; but he, too, was amazed when later on I told them of a bright red line or *scratch* on the right-hand side of my sister's face, which I distinctly had seen. When I mentioned this my mother rose trembling to her feet and nearly fainted away, and as soon as she had sufficiently recovered her self-possession, with tears streaming down her face, she exclaimed that I had indeed seen my sister, as no living mortal but herself was aware of that scratch, which she had actually made while doing some little act of kindness after my sister's death. She said she well remembered how pained she was to think she should have, unintentionally, marred the features of her dead daughter, and that, unknown to all, she had carefully obliterated all traces of the slight scratch with the aid of powder, etc., and that she had never mentioned it to a human being, from that day to this.... Yet I saw the scratch as bright as if just made...."

[Confirmatory statements were obtained from the narrator's father and brother; his mother having died in the interval.]

A GHOST IN HAMPTON COURT

Miss X. (Mrs. Hans Spoer) relates the following interesting case, as occurring to herself, on a visit to the well-known Hampton Court. (*Essays in Psychical Research*, pp. 31-34):

"I recently found myself the guest of a lady occupying a pleasant suite of rooms in Hampton Court Palace. For obvious reasons I cannot specify the name of my hostess, the exact date of my visit, or the precise whereabouts of her apartment.

"Of course I was familiar with the Hampton Court ghost legend.... I examined the scene of the occurrences, and was allowed to ask questions at will. The ghost, I was told, visited habitually in a dozen different rooms—not, however, in the bright, dainty drawing room in which we were chatting, and where it was difficult to believe that we were discussing recent history.

"As a matter of fact, it was very recent, indeed. But a few nights earlier, in a certain small but cheerful bedroom, a little girl had been awakened out of her sleep by a visitant so dramatic that I wondered whether the child had possibly gone to sleep again, after her original fright, and dreamed the later and more sensational part of the story.

"My room was quaintly pretty, but somewhat peculiar in arrangement, and lighted only from the roof. I have seen 'ghosts' before, have slept for months together in haunted houses; and, though I find such visitants somewhat exciting, I cannot say that my prospects for the night filled me with any degree of apprehension.

"At dinner and during the evening ghostly topics were avoided; there were other guests, and music and chat occupied us till 11 o'clock, when my hostess accompanied me to my room. I asked various questions as to my neighbours above and below, and the exact position of other members of the household, with a view to knowing how to interpret any sounds which might occur. About a third of the ceiling of my room was skylight; the servant's bedroom being situated over the remainder. Two sides of the room were bounded by a corridor, into which it opened; a third of the wall by the state apartments, while the fourth opened by folding doors upon a room for the time unoccupied (except by a cat, asleep upon a chair) out of which there opened a door, leading by a secret passage to the bank of the river.

"I ascertained that the folding doors were locked; moreover, a heavy table stood against them on the outer side, and a wardrobe on the inner. The bedstead was a small one, without curtains; indeed, the room contained no hangings whatever. The door into the room opened so nearly to the head of my bed that there was space only for a small table, upon which I took care to place two long candles, and a plentiful supply of matches, being somewhat addicted to late and early reading.

"I was tired, but a sense of duty demanded that I should not sleep through the 'witching hours,' so I sat up in bed, and gave my best attention to Lord Farrer's problem, 'Shall We Degrade our Standard of Value?' in the current number of the *National Review*, and, on the principle of always trying to see both sides of a question, thought of several reasons why we should not, with the author, come to a negative conclusion. The matter did not, however, excite me to the pitch of wakefulness; and when I finished the article, as the clock struck half-past one, I considered myself absolved from further responsibility, put out my lights, and was asleep before the next quarter sounded.

"Nearly three hours later I was suddenly awakened from dreamless slumber by the sound of the opening of a door against which some piece of furniture was standing, in, as it seemed, the empty room to my right. I remembered the cat, and tried to conceive by what kind of 'rampaging' she could contrive to be so noisy. A minute later there followed a thud apparently on *this* side of the folding doors, and too heavy for even the prize animals of my home circle, not to speak of a mongrel stray, newly adopted and not yet doing credit to her keep! 'A dress fallen in the wardrobe,' was my next thought, and I stretched out my hand for the match-box, as a preliminary to enquiry.

"I did not reach the matches. It seemed to me that a restraining hand was laid upon mine; I withdrew it quickly, and gazed around me in the darkness. Some minutes passed in blackness and silence. I had the sensation of a presence in the room, and finally, mindful of the tradition that a ghost should be spoken to, I said gently: 'Is anyone there? Can I do anything for you?' I remembered that the last person who entertained the ghost had said: 'Go away, I don't want you!' and I hoped that my visitor would admire my better manners and be responsive. However, there was no answer—no sound of any kind; and returning to my theory of the cat and the fallen dress, though nevertheless so far influenced by the recollection of those detaining fingers as not to attempt to strike a light, I rose and walked round my bed, keeping the right hand on the edge of the bedstead, while, with my left arm extended, I swept the surrounding space. As the room is small, I thus fairly well satisfied myself that it contained nothing unusual.

"I was, though somewhat perplexed, about to grant myself license to go to sleep again, when in the darkness before me there began to glow a soft light. I watched it increase in brightness and in extent. It seemed to radiate from a central point, which gradually took form and became a tall, slight woman, moving slowly across the room from the folding doors on my right. As she passed the foot of my bed I felt a slight vibration of the spring mattress. At the further corner she stopped, so that I had time to observe her profile and general appearance. Her face was insipidly pretty; that of a woman from thirty to thirty-five years of age, her figure slight, her dress of a soft dark material, having a full skirt and broad sash or soft waist-band tied high up, almost under her arms, a crossed or draped 'kerchief over the shoulders, sleeves which I noticed fitted very tight below the elbow, and hair which was dressed so as not to lie flat to the head, either in curls or bows, I could not tell which. As she appeared to stand between me and the light, I cannot speak with any certainty as to the color, but the dress, though dark, was, I think, not black. In spite of all this definiteness, I was, of course, conscious that the figure was unsubstantial, and I felt guilty of absurdity in asking once more: 'Will you let me help you? Can I be of use to you?'

"My voice sounded preternaturally loud, but I felt no surprise at noticing that it produced no effect upon my visitor. She stood still for perhaps two minutes—though it is very difficult to estimate time on such occasions. She then raised her hands, which were long and white, and held them before her as she sank upon her knees and slowly buried the face in her palms, in the attitude of prayer—when, quite suddenly, the light went out, and I was alone in the darkness.

"I felt that the scene was ended, the curtain down, and had no hesitation in lighting the candle at my side.

"I tried to examine the impression the vision conveyed. I felt that it was definitely that of reproach, yet of gentle resignation. There was no force, no passion; I had seen a meek, sad woman who had succumbed. I began to turn over in my mind the illustrious names of former occupants of the chamber. I fixed on one—a bad man of the worst kind, a mad fool of that time of wickedness and folly, the Regency—I thought of the secret passage in the next room, and began to weave an elaborate romance.

"'This will not do here and now,' I reflected, as the clock struck four; and, as an act of mental discipline, I returned to my *National Review*.... I turned to Mr. Myers' article on 'The Drift of Psychical Research,' which I had already seen. I read:

"'... Where telepathy operates, many intelligences may affect our own. Some of these are the minds of living persons, but some appear to be discarnate, to be spirits like ourselves, but released from the body, although still retaining much of the personality of earth. These spirits appear still to have some knowledge of our world, and to be in certain ways able to affect it.'

"Here was, so to speak, the text of my illustration. I had quite enough to think about—more than I needed for that occasion. I never heard the clock strike five!

"Let us try to examine this, a type of many ghost stories.

"Elsewhere I have classified visions of persons, whether seen in the crystal or otherwise, as:

"1. Visions of the living, clairvoyant or telepathic, usually accompanied by their own background, or adapting themselves to mine.

"2. Visions of the departed, having no obvious relations to time and space.

"3. Visions which are more or less of the nature of pictures, such as those which I voluntarily produce in the crystal from memory or imagination, or which appear in the background of real persons as illustrative of their thoughts of history. This is very often the case when an impression reaches me in visual form from the mind of a friend who, it may be, imperfectly remembers or is imperfectly informed as to the form and color of the picture his mind conveys.

"Again I emphasize the fact that I am speculating, not dogmatizing—that I am speaking from internal evidence, with no possibility of corroboration, and that I am perfectly aware that each reader must take this for what it seems to him worth. Such being the case, I venture to classify the vision under Class III. Again, to borrow from Mr. Myers, I believe that what I saw may have been a *telepathic impression of the dreams* (or I should prefer to say '*thoughts*') *of the dead*. If what I saw were indeed veridical or truth-telling—if my readers will agree to admit that what I saw was no mere illusion, or morbid hallucination, or imagination (taking the word in its commonly-accepted sense)—then I believe that my visitor was not a departed spirit, such as it has before now, perhaps, been my privilege to meet, but rather an image as such—just as the figure which, it may be, sits at my dining table is not *really* the friend whose visit a few hours later it announces, but only a representation of him, having no objective existence apart from the truth of the information it conveys—a thought which is personal to the brain which thinks it.

"I have already said that, preconceived notions apart, I had no impression of reality. I recognized that what I saw and felt was an externalization of impressions unconsciously received, possibly from some discarnate mind...."

— HEREWARD CARRINGTON —

HALF-PAST ONE O'CLOCK

The following case is in many ways classical. Mrs. Claughton, to whom the experience came, was a widowed lady, living in good social circles. The full account of her experience is to be found in the *Proceedings* of the Society for Psychical Research (Vol. XI., pp. 547-59), and contains statements and personal investigations by Dr. Ferrier, Andrew Lang, Mr. Myers and the Marquis of Bute as well as corroborative testimony from the Clerk at Meresby, Mrs. Claughton's governess, copies of letters, diaries, memoranda, etc. The whole case is very complicated and impressive; and embodies a combination of apparent spirit communication, clairvoyance, telepathy, precognition, apparitions, and supernormal dreams. The chief and most interesting account is the statement made by Mrs. Claughton to the Marquis of Bute, and recorded by him as follows:

"She was staying in 1893 with her two children at 6 Blake St., a house belonging to Mrs. Appleby, daughter of the late Mrs. Blackburn ... but let to Mrs. Buckley. She had heard the house was haunted, and may have heard that the ghost was Mrs. Blackburn's. She had been told also that water was spilt on the floors inexplicably. They arrived on October 4th. About 1.15 a.m., Monday, October 9th, Mrs. Claughton was in bed with one of her children, the other sleeping in the room. Mrs. Claughton had offered to be of any use she could to Miss Buckley, who had arrived from London on the Saturday, not feeling very well. She had been asleep, and was awakened by the footsteps of a person coming downstairs, whom she supposed to be a servant coming to call her. The steps stopped at the door. The sounds were repeated twice more at the interval of a few moments. Mrs. Claughton rose, lit the candle, and opened the door. There was no one there. She noticed the clock outside pointed to 1.20 a.m. She shut the door, got into bed, read, and, leaving the candle burning, went to sleep. Woke up, finding the candle spluttering out. Heard a sound like a sigh. Saw a woman standing by the bed. She had a soft white shawl round the shoulders, held by the right hand towards the left shoulder, bending slightly forwards. Mrs. Claughton thinks the hair was lightish brown, and the shawl partly over the head, but does not remember distinctly, and has no impression of the rest of the dress; it was not grave-clothes. She said: 'Follow me.' Mrs. Claughton rose, took the candle, and followed her out of the room, across the passage, and into the drawing-room. She had no recollection as to the opening of the doors. The house maid next day declared that the drawing-room door had been locked by her. On entering the drawing-room, Mrs. Claughton, finding the candle on the point of extinction, replaced it by a pink one from the chiffonier near the door. The figure nearly at the end of the room, turned three-quarters round, said 'to-morrow,' and disappeared. Mrs. Claughton returned to the bedroom, where she found her elder child (not the one in the bed) sitting up. It asked: 'Who is the lady in white?' Mrs. Claughton thinks she answered the child: 'It's only me—mother; go to sleep,' or the like words, and hushed her to sleep in her arms. The baby remained fast asleep. She lit the gas and remained awake for some two hours, then put out the lights and went to sleep. Had no fear while seeing the figure, but was upset after seeing it. Would not be prepared to swear that she might not have walked in her sleep. Pink candle, partly burned, in her room in morning. Does not know if she took it burnt or new.

"In the morning she spoke to Mr. Buckley, on whose advice she went to ask Dr. Ferrier as to the figure about 3 p.m. He and his wife said the description was like that of Mrs. Blackburn, whom Mrs. Claughton already suspected it to be. Thinks Dr. Ferrier already told her that Miss Blackburn (Mrs. Appleby) had seen her mother in the same house. Mrs. Claughton cannot recognize the photograph of Mrs. Blackburn shown to her by Mr. Y. (who got it from Mrs. M.). She says the figure seemed smaller, and the features were more pinched and attenuated, like those of a person in the last stages of consumption, which was also the general appearance. By his advice, Mr. Buckley put an electric bell under Mrs. Claughton's pillow, communicating with Miss Buckley's room, as Mrs. Claughton determined to sit up that night and watch.

"That night Mrs. Claughton sat up dressed, with the gas burning. About 12 she partly undressed, put on a dressing gown, and lay down outside the bed, gas still burning, and fell asleep reading. Woke up and found the same woman as before, but the expression even more agitated. She bent over Mrs. Claughton and said: 'I have come, listen.' She then made a certain statement and asked Mrs. Claughton to do certain things. Mrs. Claughton said: 'Am I dreaming, or is it true?' The figure said something like: 'If you doubt me, you will find that the date of my marriage was * * *.' (This was the date of the marriage, which took place in India, of Mrs. Blackburn to Mr. Blackburn, who is alive and married again. Mrs. Claughton first learned the corroboration of the date from Dr. Ferrier on the following Thursday). After this Mrs. Claughton saw a man standing on Mrs. B.'s left hand—tall, dark, well made, healthy, sixty years old, or more, ordinary man's day clothes, kind, good expression. A conversation ensued between the three, in course of which man stated himself to be George Howard, buried in Meresby Churchyard (Mrs. Claughton had never heard of Meresby or of George Howard) and gave the date of his marriage * * * and death * * *. [Entries of these dates seen by me in Mrs. Claughton's pocketbook, as torn out and lent to me. F. W. H. Myers.] He desired Mrs. Claughton to go to Meresby and verify these dates in the registration, and, if found correct, to go to the church at the ensuing 1.15 a.m. and wait at the grave therein (S. W. corner of S. aisle) of Richard Hart, died * * *, ætat * * *. She was to verify this reference also in the registers. He said her railway ticket would not be taken, and she was to send it along with a white rose from his grave to Dr. Ferrier. Forbade her having any previous communication with the place, or going in her own name. Said Joseph Wright, a dark man, to whom she should describe him, would help her. That she would lodge with a woman who would tell her that she had a child (drowned) buried in the same churchyard. When Mrs. Claughton had done all this, she should hear the rest of the history. Towards the end of the conversation, Mrs. Claughton saw a third phantom, that of a man whose name she is not free to give, in great trouble, standing, with hands on face (which he afterwards lowered, showing face) behind Mrs. Blackburn's right. The three disappeared. Mrs. Claughton rose and went to the door to look out at the clock, but was seized with faintness, returned and rang the electric bell. Mr. Buckley found her on the ground. She was able to ask the time, which was about 1.20 a.m. Then fainted, and the Buckleys undressed her and put her to bed.

"That morning, Tuesday, Mrs. Claughton sent for Dr. Ferrier, who corroborated certain matters so far as she asked him, and ascertained for her the date of Mrs. Blackburn's marriage (she received his note of the date on Thursday). She went to the Post Office, and found that Meresby existed. Returned, and ascertained that it was in Suffolk, and so wrote that evening to Dr. Ferrier, and went to London with her daughters that (Thursday) evening.

"Friday night, Mrs. Claughton dreamt that she arrived at 5, after dusk, that a fair was going on, and that she had to go to place after place to get lodgings. Also, she and her eldest daughter dreamt that she would fail if she did not go alone. Went to Station for

12 noon train on Saturday. Went to refreshment room for luncheon, telling porter to call her in time. He went by mistake to waiting room, and she missed train and had to wait (going to the British Museum, where she wrote her name in Jewel room) until 3.5, as stated. House where she finally found lodgings was that of Joseph Wright, who turned out to be the parish clerk. She sent for the curate by porter, to ask as to consulting registers, but as he was dining out he did not come till after she had gone to bed. Sunday morning, Mrs. Wright spoke to her about the drowned child buried in the churchyard. Went to forenoon service, and immediately afterwards went into vestry and verified the registers; described George Howard to Joseph Wright, who had known him and recognized description; then was taken by Joseph Wright to the graves of Richard Hart and George Howard. On the latter there is no stone, but three mounds surrounded by a railing overgrown with white roses. She gathered rose for Dr. Ferrier, as had been directed. Walked and talked with curate, who was not sympathetic. After luncheon went with Mrs. Wright and walked round Howard's house (country house in park). Attended evening service, and afterwards, while, watching the lights put out and the church furniture covered up, wondered if she would have the nerve to go on. Back to supper, afterwards slept and had dream of a terrorizing character, whereof has full written description. Dark night, hardly any moon, a few stars. To church with Joseph Wright at 1 a.m., with whom searched interior and found it empty. At 1.20 a.m. was locked in alone,

having no light; had been told to take Bible, but had only church-service, which she had left in vestry in the morning. Waited near grave of Richard Hart; felt no fear. Received communication, but does not feel free to give any detail; no light. History begun at Blake street then completed. Was directed to take another white rose from George Howard's grave and gathered rose for Miss Howard, as had been directed. Home and bed, and slept well for the first time since first seeing Mrs. Blackburn.

"Next day went and sketched church and identified grave of Mrs. Rose, on whose grave, she had been told in church, she would find a message for herself. The words engraved were * * *.

"Then called on Miss Howard and recognized strong likeness to her father. Carried out all things desired by the dead to the full, as had been requested. Has had no communication from any of them since. Nothing since has appeared in Blake street. The wishes expressed to her were not illogical or unreasonable, as the ratiocination of dreams often appears, but perfectly rational, reasonable, and of natural importance."

MY OWN TRUE GHOST STORY

The following narrative was told to me by a very well-known artist; who maintains the strict accuracy of every word in his account, as given below:

"I had been living in Paris for some months when I decided to change my quarters, and move into a studio more in keeping with my present allowance. After a brief search, I saw one which exactly suited me. It was a large room, at the end of a long, dark rambling passage, with doors leading into other studios on either side all the way down. As my neighbours turned out to be a very jolly, happy crew, I liked the life immensely, and everything promised well for the new abode.

"I had been there for, perhaps, two weeks when I had my first 'ghostly' adventure. I had been out rather late, having had late supper, and perhaps a little too much wine for my best health. At the same time, I was absolutely sober, and in full possession of all my senses. I felt a little happy and convivial—that was all.

"Walking along the passage, I was approaching my door when I distinctly heard the rustle of a silk skirt walking down the passage ahead of me. As the hallway was dark, I could not see whether or not the girl was just in front of me, or some distance away. It never for a moment struck me that it was not a flesh-and-blood visitant. My only thought was: One of the boys has been having a little supper, and this must be one of his visitors going home. I called aloud: 'Mayn't I strike a light and show you the way along this dark hall?' And, suiting the action to the word, I struck a match, and held it up over my head. Nothing was visible! I peered into vacancy; no female figure could I see. I listened for the sound of steps, or the swish of a silken petticoat; but not a sound could I hear. I walked along the passage; not a sign of life was anywhere manifest. Everything was dark, lonely and deserted.

"I came to the conclusion that I must have been deceived; and thought no more about it. I went to bed and to sleep.

"It was, perhaps, two nights later when the same thing occurred. Coming home, about 10 o'clock at night, I heard the same swish of the skirt; the same soft, feminine footsteps. This time the hall was light, and I could *see* that no one was there. I recalled the incident of the other evening, and a cold chill began to creep up my backbone. I entered my room, however, lit the lamp, leaving my door open. 'Now,' thought I, 'if anyone passes that door again, I shall surely see them.' I put on a dressing gown and a pair of slippers, and sat down to read—facing the door.

"Perhaps five minutes had elapsed when I saw the door very slowly open still further on its hinges. A moment later I felt in the room a 'Presence,' which I distinctly felt to be that of a young woman, about twenty years of age. So vivid was the mental picture I formed of this person that her very features and coloring were sensed by me—though, of course, I had no means of knowing whether or not I was right.

"The Presence glided across the room, and sat itself upon the edge of my sofa, about three feet distant from where I sat. I looked at the spot intently, and felt that the eyes of my invisible visitor were upon me, regarding me intently, as though studying my character to the best of her ability. She had a comfortable sort of feeling about her, which made me seem at once at home with her; so that, without further ceremony, I said to the Presence: 'Pray make yourself at home. If

I can do anything for you, let me know.'

"I waited, but of course there was no response. Only I thought I caught again the faintest rustle of silk, as the figure seated itself in a more comfortable position. I put down my book, and began to paint. The feeling of loneliness, which I had experienced ever since my removal into the new studio, vanished immediately. I felt that a living, human—if invisible—being was with me, watching my work and keeping me company during the long hours of discouragement and unproductive effort.

"Several times, during the course of the evening, I spoke to the Presence; but received no reply. Only I felt its proximity, and knew when the figure changed its position, as it did once or twice. Once it came over and stood by my side, as though looking at the canvas, and criticising it with me. Then it went back to its seat at the end of the sofa.

"Bed time came. I felt almost abashed to go to bed with this feminine presence in the room! However, as there was nothing left for me to do, I undressed, got into bed, and blew out the light. The Presence came over and sat on the side of my bed. When I went to sleep, it was still sitting there.

"The next morning it had gone. I felt inexpressibly lonely. I missed the Presence, whom I now began to call 'Her' instead of 'It,' and wished she would return and keep me company! It did not do so, however, until the following evening, when, about nine o'clock, I again felt her approach, felt her entrance through my studio door, and felt her seat herself in my easy chair, and turn her eyes upon me. I knew that she was regarding me intently—perhaps critically—and I felt almost angry that I, in turn, could not see her. I gazed at the chair *determined* to see her; but nothing save empty space met my gaze! With a gesture of impatience and irritation, I turned away, and went on with my painting.

"Presently, I was aware that She was standing beside me, examining the painting upon the easel. 'Well, do you like it?' I said almost caustically. The Presence immediately returned and sat in the chair, and I knew that I had offended Her. I threw my brush and pallet aside and apologized. So she came and stood by me again; and again she remained with me until I closed my eyes in sleep.

"This sort of thing went on for several weeks. Every evening the Presence visited me, kept me company, making the day seem long and dreary until she came. I waited for her appearance with growing impatience. I could never see or feel anything; my spoken words brought no response; yet there she was; and I felt just as assured of the presence, in my studio, of a feminine spiritual being as of my own existence. Every evening the Presence was with me when I went to sleep; every morning it had vanished. The sense of friendliness and companionship was complete and unmistakable.

"One evening my visitor failed to appear! I could do no work; I paced the floor, I could do nothing, think of nothing! The sense of desolation and loneliness was absolute. I hardly realized, until then, how completely I had grown accustomed to the presence of my invisible visitor. I missed her more than I ever dreamed I could miss anyone in life. Forlorn and forsaken, I went to bed, and finally dropped into a fitful and broken sleep.

"For about a week things went on in this way. I had grown gradually reconciled to my lonely life, and was painting hard for an exhibition which was near at hand. One evening I came into the studio, and I found the Presence waiting for me—seated in the easy chair, by the fire.

"I felt my heart and whole being give a throb of joy and recognition—just as it would at the sight of an old and very dear friend. I knew how much I had missed her! I knew that She had risen, and was standing, facing me, as I entered. Before I had time to check myself, or think what I was doing, I had rushed forward, crying 'Dearest,' with outstretched arms, and had embraced the spot where I knew her to be standing! I grasped the empty air, but I somehow felt two hands placed upon my shoulders, and the imprint of a delicate kiss upon my lips.

"I no longer felt lonely. I whistled, I sang, I took off my coat, and, donning jacket and slippers, set to work with joy upon my picture. I painted hard, and all the while the Presence stood by me, criticising—approving or disapproving—and in every instance I felt Her criticism and judgment to be right.

"A year went by. I had to give up my studio, and return to America, on my father's sudden death. The parting with the Presence I shall never forget. Had two lovers in the flesh parted from one another, it could not have been more real, more touching, more sincere. For my own part I was heartbroken. The Presence, too, I knew to be weeping. The parting was long and sorrowful. Finally, I tore myself away.

"I have never seen or felt anything from that day to this. But of the reality and objective existence of that Presence I am as assured as I am of any event in my life. No one can tell me that it was a trick of the imagination—I know better! She was as real to me as any personality I have ever known. Yes, the Unreal is Real, of that I have no doubt whatever. My own experience with the Ghostly world has proved that to *my* satisfaction!"

CHAPTER IV

HAUNTED HOUSES

When "phantasms of the dead" constantly appear in one house, and there only, that house is said to be "haunted" and, in such a case, the phantasms seem to be attracted to the *locality* more than to the individuals living in it. This is usually the case in so-called haunted houses; no matter *who* lives within them, they one and all see the spectral forms; but this is not invariably so. In the case of the "Great Amherst Mystery," for example—given below—the haunting seemed to be associated with the *person* more than the *house*, so that we might be said to have here a case of a Haunted Man (or Woman). But this is the exception, not the rule.

The cases that follow are all well-attested; and the phenomena have been witnessed by many persons. The original Reports, for the most part, have appeared in the *Proceedings* of the S. P. R., and the facts were carefully investigated at the time, by competent investigators. The first instance is particularly interesting, because of the experiments which were tried to ascertain the nature of the "ghost," and if many more such experiments were conducted, we might hope, in time, to know something about them. I shall begin with a carefully recorded example, which I may call—

THE RECORD OF A HAUNTED HOUSE

The case of a haunted house here given is very well authenticated, and corroborated by six written and signed statements, as well as that of the original informant. The account originally appeared in the *Proceedings* of the S. P. R., Vol. VIII., pp. 311-32, and is drawn up by Miss Morton, a lady of scientific training who resided for a long time in the house in question. She was well-known to Mr. Myers, then Hon. Sec. of the Society. Very interesting experiments were conducted to test the nature of the "ghost" as the following brief account will show:

"My father took the house in March, 1882, none of us having then heard of anything unusual about the house. We moved in towards the end of April, and it was not until the following June that I first saw the apparition.

"I had gone up to my room, but was not yet in bed, when I heard someone at the door, and went to it, thinking it might be my mother. On opening the door, I saw no one; but on going a few steps along the passage I saw the figure of a tall lady, dressed in black, standing at the head of the stairs. After a few moments she descended the stairs, and I followed for a short distance, feeling curious what it could be. I had only a small piece of candle, and it suddenly burnt itself out; and, being unable to see more, I went back to my room.

"On the night of August 2, the footsteps were heard by my three sisters and by the cook, all of whom slept on the top landing—also by my married sister, Mrs. K., who was sleeping on the floor below. They all said the next morning that they had heard them very plainly pass and repass their doors.... These footsteps are very characteristic, and are not at all like those of any people in the house; they are soft and rather slow, though decided and even. My sisters would not go out on the landing after hearing them pass, but each time when I have gone out after hearing them, I have seen the figure there.

"On the evening of August 1, we were sitting in the drawing-room, with the gas lit but the shutters not shut, the light outside getting dusk—my brothers and a friend having just given up tennis, finding it too dark; my elder sister, Mrs. E., and myself both saw the figure on the balcony outside, looking in at the window. She stood there some minutes, then walked to the end and back again, after which she seemed to disappear. She soon after came into the drawing-room, when I saw her, but my sister did not.

"The apparitions were (always) of exactly the same type, seen in the same places by the same people, at varying intervals.

"The footsteps continued, and were heard by several visitors and new servants, who had taken the places of those who had left, as well as by myself, four sisters and brothers; in all by about twenty people, many of them not having previously heard of the apparitions and sounds.

"Other sounds were also heard in addition which seemed gradually to increase in intensity. They consisted in walking up and down on the second floor landing, of bumps against the doors of the bedrooms, and of the handles of the doors turning. The bumps against the doors were so marked as to terrify a new servant, who had heard nothing of the haunting, into the belief that burglars were breaking into her room....

"During the year, at Mr. Myers' suggestion, I kept a photographic camera constantly ready to try to photograph the figure, but on the few occasions I was able to do so, I got no result; at night, usually only by candle light, a long exposure would be necessary for so dark a figure, and this I could not obtain.

"I also tried to communicate with the figure, constantly speaking to it and asking it to make signs, if not able to speak, but with no result. I also tried especially to *touch* her, but did not succeed. On cornering her, as I did once or twice, she vanished.

"One night, my sister E. went up to her room on the second story, but as she passed the room where my two sisters L. and M. were sleeping, they opened their door to say that they had heard noises, and also seen what they described as a *flame* of a candle, without candle or handle visible, cross the room diagonally from corner to corner. Two of the maids opened the doors of their two bedrooms, and said that they also heard noises; they all 5 stood at their doors with their lighted candles for some little time. They all heard steps walking up and down the landing between them; as they passed they felt a sensation which they described as a 'cold wind' though their candles were not blown out. They saw nothing. The steps then descended the stairs, re-ascended, again descended, and did not return....

"The figure became much less substantial on its later appearances. Up to about 1886 it was so solid and life-like that it was often mistaken for a real person. It gradually became less distinct. At all times it intercepted the light; we have not been able to ascertain if it cast a shadow. I should mention that it has been seen through window glass, and that I myself wear glasses habitually, though none of the other percipients do so. The upper part of the figure always left a more distinct impression than the lower, but this may partly be due to the fact that one naturally looks at people's faces before their feet.

PROOFS OF IMMATERIALITY

"1. I have several times fastened fine strings across the stairs at various heights before going to bed, but after all others have gone up to their rooms.... I have twice, at least, seen the figure pass through the cords, leaving them intact.

"2. The sudden and complete disappearance of the figure while still in full view.

"3. The impossibility of touching the figure....

"4. It has appeared in a room with the doors shut.

CONDUCT OF ANIMALS IN THE HOUSE

"We have strong grounds for believing that the apparition was seen by two dogs. "Twice I remember seeing our dog suddenly run up to the mat at the footof the stairs in the hall, wagging his tail, and moving his back in the way dogs do when expecting to be caressed. It jumped up, fawning as it would do if a person was standing there, but suddenly slunk away with its tail between its legs, and retreated, trembling, under a sofa. We were all strongly under the impression that it had seen the figure. Its action was peculiar, and was much more striking to an onlooker than it could possibly appear from a description.

"In conclusion, as to the feelings aroused by the presence of the figure, it is very difficult to describe them; on the first few occasions, I think the feeling of awe at something unknown, mixed with a strong desire to know more about it, predominated. Later, when I was able to analyze my feelings more closely, and the first novelty had gone off, I was conscious of a feeling of *loss*, as if I had lost power to the figure.

"Most of the other percipients speak of a feeling of cold wind, but I myself have not experienced this...."

B—— HOUSE

This is a very famous case of "Haunting," which was investigated by Sir Oliver Lodge, Mr. F. W. H. Myers, Colonel Taylor (a specialist on Haunted Houses), Miss X., the Marquis of Bute, etc. The chief reports of the occurrence are due to the last three named persons; and from the Journal kept during their occupancy of the house the following extracts are made:

"*February 4, Thursday*. I awoke suddenly, just before 3 a.m. Miss Moore, who had been lying awake for over two hours, said: 'I want you to stay awake and listen.' Almost immediately I was startled by a loud clanging sound, which seemed to resound through the house. The mental image it brought to my mind was as of a long metal bar, such as I have seen near iron-foundries, being struck at intervals with a wooden mallet. The noise was distinctly that of metal struck with wood; it seemed to come diagonally across the house. It sounded very loud, though distinct, and the idea that any inmate of the house should not hear it seemed preposterous....

"I also had an experience this morning which may have been purely subjective, but which should be recorded. About 10 a.m., I was writing in the library, face to light, back to fire. Mrs. W. was in the room, and addressed me once or twice; but I was aware of not being responsive, as I was much occupied. I wrote on, and presently felt a distinct, but gentle push against my chair. I thought it was the dog, and looked down, but he was not there. I went on writing, and in a few minutes felt a push, firm and decided, against myself which moved me on my chair. I thought it was Mrs. W——, who, having spoken and obtained no answer, was reminding me of her presence. I looked backward with an exclamation—the room was empty! She came in presently, and called my attention to the dog, who was gazing intently from the hearth-rug at the place where I had expected (before) to see him....

"As the day began with the above, and as I had had a quiet rest, I went to 'the copse' at dusk. The moon was bright, and the twilight lingered. We waited about in the avenue to let it get darker, but it was still far from dark. Then we made our way up to the glen—Miss Moore, Miss Langton and myself.

"I saw 'Ishbel' and 'Marget' in the old spot across the burn. [Two 'spirits' who had been seen about the house, several times before].

'Ishbel' was on her knees in the attitude of weeping, 'Marget' apparently reasoning with her in a low voice, to which 'Ishbel' replied very occasionally. I could not hear what was said from the noise of the burn. We waited for perhaps ten or fifteen minutes. They had appeared when I had been there for three or four. When we regained the avenue (in silence) Miss Moore asked Miss Langton, 'What did you see?' (She had been told nothing, except that the Colonel, who did not know details then, had said in her presence something about 'a couple of nuns.') She said: 'I saw nothing, but I heard a low talking.' Questioned further, she said it seemed close behind. The glen is so narrow that this might be quite consistent with what I heard and saw. Miss Moore heard a murmuring voice, and is quite certain it was not the burn. She is less suggestible than almost any one I know.... The dog ran up while we were there, pointed, and ran straight for the two women. He afterwards left us, and we found him barking in the glen. He is a dog who hardly ever barks. We went up among the trees where he was, and could find no cause....

"This morning's phenomenon is the most incomprehensible I have yet known. I heard the banging sounds after we were in bed last night. Early this morning, about 5.30, I was awakened by them. They continued for nearly an hour. Then another sound began *in* the room. It might have been made by a very lively kitten jumping and pouncing, or even by a very large bird; there was a fluttering noise too.[3] It was close, exactly opposite the bed. Miss Moore woke up, and we heard the noise going on till nearly eight o'clock. I drew up the blinds and opened the windows wide. I sought all over the room, looking into cupboards and under furniture. We cannot guess at any possible explanation...."

A few weeks later, Miss X., wrote in her "Journal":

"The general tone of things is disquieting, and new in our experience. Hitherto, in our first occu-

---

[3] This fluttering noise, as of a bird, is very often met with in the literature of the occult, and is typical of 'haunted houses.' In the famous case of Lord Lyttleton, for instance, this was recorded, and was said to announce his death. He died three days later, in bed.

pation, the phenomena affected one as melancholy, depressing and perplexing, but now all, quite independently, say the same thing—that the influence is evil and horrible—even poor little 'Spooks' (the dog) who was never terrified before, has been since our return here. The worn faces at breakfast are really a dismal sight."

Soon after this the investigators left the house.

WILLINGTON MILL

This is one of the most famous Haunted Houses on record. The case has been described in various books on ghosts, the most complete account being that contained in the *Journal* of the Psychical Research Society.... Mr. Proctor lived for several years in the haunted mill, and got quite used to the apparitions, which stalked about the place at all hours. Visitors, however, did not like them as much as he did. The following extracts will suffice to explain the general character of the haunting in this case—

"When two of Mrs. Proctor's sisters were staying at the Mill on a visit, their bed was suddenly violently shaken, the curtains hoisted up all round to their tester and then as rapidly let down again, and this again in rapid succession. The curtains were taken off the next night, with the result that they both saw a female figure, of mysterious substance and of a greyish-blue hue come out of the wall at the head of the bed and lean over them. They both saw it distinctly. They saw it come out of and go back again into the wall.... Mrs.

Davidson's sister-in-law had a curious experience on one occasion. One evening she was putting one of the bedrooms right, and, looking toward the dressing table, saw what she supposed was a white towel lying on the ground. She went to pick it up, but imagine her surprise when she found that it rose up, and went up behind the dressing-table over the top, down on the floor across the room, disappeared under the door, and was heard to descend the stairs with a heavy step! The noise which it made in doing so was distinctly heard by Mr. Proctor and others in the house.

"On one occasion, Mr. Mann, the old mill foreman, with his wife and daughter, and Mrs. Proctor's sister, all four saw the figure of a bald headed old man in a flowing robe like a surplice gliding backwards and forwards about three feet from the floor, level with the bottom of the second story window; he then stood still in the middle of the window and part of the body which appeared quite luminous showed through the blind. While in that position, the framework of the window was visible, while the body was as brilliant as a star, and diffused a radiance all round; then it turned a bluish tinge, and gradually faded away from the head downwards.

"The children, however, were the chief ghost-seers. On one occasion one of the little girls came to Mrs. Davidson and said: 'There is a lady sitting on the bed in mamma's bedroom. She has eyeholes but no eyes; and she looked so hard at me.' On another occasion a boy of two years old was charmed with the ghost, and laughed and kicked, crying out: 'Ah dares somebody—pee, pee!' On one occasion the mother saw through the bed curtain a figure cross the room to the table on which the light was burning, take up the snuffers and snuff the candle....

"Several experiments were made with a clairvoyant by the name of Jane, to ascertain the cause of the mystery. In the mesmeric trance she described the house accurately; described the nature of the disturbances which were going on within it; and stated that the chief cause of the trouble was to be found 'in the cellar.' This was not verified. The full story, as narrated, is certainly one of the most curious to be found anywhere."

THE GREAT AMHERST MYSTERY

This is one of the most remarkable cases on record. It is the case of a haunted house, in which many *physical* manifestations of all sorts took place, and were observed by nearly a hundred persons, all of whom testified as to the reality of the facts. The house in question is situated in Amherst, N. S.—hence the name. Residing in this small house were (when the events occurred) Mr. and Mrs. Teed, their children, Willie, aged five years, and George, aged seventeen months. His wife's two sisters, Jennie and Esther Cox, also lived with them—Esther being the person around whom nearly all the phenomena centered. John Teed and William Cox also boarded at the house—brothers of Mr. and Mrs. Teed, respectively.

The manifestations began in a very peculiar manner. The two girls, who had just gone to bed (they slept together) were on the point of falling asleep, when Esther suddenly jumped out of bed with a scream, exclaiming that there was a mouse in the mattress. A careful search failed, however, to reveal the presence of any mouse. The same thing happened the next night; and when the girls got up to search for the mouse, a paste-board box, which was under the bed, jumped up in the air and fell over on its side. They decided to say nothing about it; got into bed again, and were soon asleep.

The next night manifestations began in earnest. Esther began to swell; her body became puffed all over, and she thought she was going to burst. She screamed with pain. Just then, however, three terrific reports shook the room, and the swelling suddenly subsided. She was placed in bed; but no sooner had she been placed upon it than all the bed-clothes flew off her, and settled in the far corner of the room. "They could see them passing through the air by the light of the kerosene lamp which was lighted and standing on the table, and both screamed as only scared girls can, and then Jennie fainted."

The bed-clothes were replaced. No sooner was this done than the pillow flew out from under her head, and landed in the center of the floor. It was replaced, but again flew out, hitting Mr. Teed in the face. Three deafening reports then shook the house; after which all manifestations ceased for the night.

The next night, these manifestations were repeated; the bed-clothes flew off, in view of all; and in the midst of this, the sound of scratching became audible, as of a metallic object scraping plaster. "All looked at the wall whence the sound of writing came, when, to their great astonishment, there could be plainly read these words: 'Esther Cox, you are mine to kill.' Every person in the room could see the writing plainly, and yet but a moment before nothing was to be seen but the plain kalsomined wall!...

These things continued day after day, and were seen by many persons. Articles would be thrown about the house; Dr. Carrittee, the family physician, saw "a bucket of cold water become agitated, and, to all appearances, boil while standing on the kitchen table." A voice was heard, in the atmosphere of the house, talking to Esther; and telling her all manner of horrible things. Soon after this, to the consternation of all present, "all saw a lighted match fall from the ceiling to the bed, having come out of the air, which would certainly have set the bed-clothing on fire, had not Jennie put it out instantly. During the next two minutes, eight or ten lighted matches fell on the bed and about the room, out of the air, but were all extinguished before anything could be set fire by them...."

This fire-raising continued for several days. The family would smell smoke, and, on running up into the bedroom, they would find a bundle of clothes placed in the center of the floor, blazing. Or they would descend to the cellar; and there find a pile of shavings alight and blazing merrily. They lived in constant danger of having the house burned over their heads.

Soon after this, things got so bad that Esther Cox had to leave home, and went to visit a friend by the name of White, in the hope that the manifestations would cease, when she was removed from her own home. For four weeks things went well; then they began again just as ever. Knocks and raps were heard all over the house, which answered questions asked them; and told the amount of money people had in their pockets, etc. Articles of furniture were thrown about; voices sounded; and, worst of all, Esther now began to *see* the ghost; and described it to those about her. Among other terrifying phenomena, which took place at Mr. Whites' house, the following should be mentioned—

"... A clasp-knife belonging to little Frederic White was taken from his hand, while he was whittling something, by the devilish ghost, who instantly stabbed Esther in the back with it, leaving the knife sticking in the wound, which was bleeding profusely. Frederic pulled the bloody knife from the wound, wiped it, closed it and put it in his pocket, which he had no sooner done than the ghost obtained possession of it again and, quick as a flash of lightning, stuck it into the same wound...."

Some person tried the experiment of placing three or four large iron spikes on Esther's lap while she was seated in the dining-saloon. To the unutterable astonishment of Mr. White, Frederic and other persons present, the spikes were not instantly removed, as it was expected they would be, but, instead, remained on her lap until they became too hot to be handled with comfort, when they were thrown by the ghost to the far end of the saloon—a distance of twenty feet. This fact was fully corroborated.

It was at this stage of the proceedings that the spot was visited by Walter Hubbell, an actor, who remained some time in Amherst, studying the case, and who has written a whole book about it—"The Great Amherst Mystery." On the night of his arrival, they all sat round a table, in full light, to see what they could see, and knocks and raps resounded immediately. "We could all hear even the scratching sound of invisible human finger nails, and the dull sounds produced by the hands, as they rubbed the table, and struck it with invisible, clenched fists, in knocking in response to questions."

The next day, Mr. Hubbell records the following facts, among others: "I had been seated about five minutes when, to my great astonishment, my umbrella was thrown a distance of sixteen feet, passing over my head in its strange flight, and almost at the same instant a large carving knife came whizzing through the air, passing over Esther's head, who was just then coming out of the pantry with a large dish in both hands, and fell in front of her, near me—having come from behind her out of the pantry. I naturally went to the door and looked in, but no person was there.

"After dinner I lay down on the sofa in the parlor; Esther was in the room seated near the center in a rocking chair. I did not sleep, but lay with my eyes only partially closed so that I could see her. While lying there a large glass paper-weight, weighing fully a pound, came whizzing through the air from a corner of the room, where I had previously noticed it on an ornamental shelf, a distance of some twelve or fifteen feet from the sofa. Had it struck my head, I should surely have been killed, so great was the force with which it was thrown....

"On Monday, June 23, they commenced again with great violence. At breakfast, the lid of the sugar bowl was heard to fall on the floor. Mrs. Teed, Esther and myself searched for it for fully five minutes, and had abandoned our search as useless, when all three saw it fall from the ceiling. I saw it, just before it fell, and it was at the moment suspended in the air about one foot from the ceiling. No one was within five feet of it at the time. The table knives were then thrown upon the floor, the chairs pitched over, and after breakfast the dining-table fell over on its side, rugs upon the floor were slid about, and the whole room literally turned into a pandemonium, so filled with dust that I went into the parlor. Just as I got inside the parlor door a large flower pot, containing a plant in full bloom, was taken from among Jennie's flowers on the stand near the window; and in a second, a tin pail, with a handle, was brought half-filled with water from the kitchen and placed beside the plant on the floor, both in the center of the parlor, and put there by a ghost. Just think of such a thing happening while the sun was shining, and only a few minutes before I had seen this same tin pail from the dining-room hanging on a nail in the kitchen, empty! And yet people say, and thousands believe, that there are no haunted houses! What a great mistake they make in so asserting; but then they never lived in a genuine one, where there was an invisible power that had full and complete sway. By all the demons! When I read the accounts now in my 'Journal,' from which my experience is copied, I am almost speechless with wonder that I ever lived to behold such sights....

"On this same day, Esther's face was slapped by the ghosts, so that the marks of fingers could be plainly seen—just exactly as if a human hand had slapped her face; these slaps could be plainly heard by all present. I heard them distinctly, time and again....

"On Thursday, June 26, Jennie and Esther told me that the night before Bob, the demon, had been in their room again. They stated he had stuck them with pins and marked them from head to foot with crosses. I saw some of the crosses, which were bloody marks, scratched upon their hands, necks and arms. It was a sad sight. During the entire day, I was busy pulling pins out of Esther; they came out of the air from all quarters, and were stuck into all the exposed portions of her person, even the head, and inside of her ears. Maggie, the ghost, took quite an interest in me, and came to my room at night, while the lamp was burning, and knocked on the headboard of my bed and on the wall near the bed, which was *not* next to the room occupied by the girls, but on an outside wall facing the stable. I carried on a most interesting conversation with her, asking a great many questions which were answered by knocks....

"A trumpet was heard in the house all day. The sound came from within the atmosphere—I can give no other description of its effect on our sense of hearing.... I wish to state, most emphatically, that I could tell the difference in the knocks made by each ghost just as well as if they had spoken. The knocks made by Maggie were delicate and soft, as if made by a woman's hand, while those made by Bob Nickle were loud and strong, denoting great strength and evidently large hands. When he knocked with those terrible sledge-hammer blows, he certainly must have used a large rock or some other heavy object, for such loud knocks were not produced with hard knuckles...."

In July the phenomena became so bad that the landlord came and told the Teed family that either Esther would have to go, or they would all have to leave the house. It was decided that Esther should go, which she did, visiting some friends by the name of Van Amburgh. From the time she left her home the second time, she was never afterwards troubled with the ghosts. Some years later, she married and went to live in another town—where she was interviewed by the present writer in 1907.

This account was sworn to by Mr. Hubbell before a notary public, and he asserts under oath that every word of the account is true. He has also produced the written confirmatory testimony of a score of still-living witnesses of the phenomena in Amherst.

A very similar case occurred in Tennessee, in 1818, and is recorded in full by M. V. Ingram, in his book, "The Bell Witch." Many other cases of a like nature are to be found in the "History of the Supernatural."

> *For ghosts of the dead*
> *Through Infinite ages*
> *Have wandered and lurked*
> *In earth's atmosphere;*
> *Watchful and eager*
> *For victims to torture*
> *To follow and kill,*
> *Or make tremble with fear.*
> *Yes, ghosts of the dead*
> *Revengeful and evil,*
> *Still come in hordes*
> *From the Stygian shore;*
> *Entering houses*
> *To torment our maidens*
> *Burning and wrecking*
> *Our homes evermore.*

BROOK HOUSE

The following case is given in full by Mr. W. T. Stead in his *Real Ghost Stories*, and I extract from his narrative some of the most striking and interesting passages. It is a truly remarkable narrative, well worthy of careful perusal.

Mr. Ralph Hastings, of Broadmeadow, Teignmouth, wrote in October, 1891, enclosing the following extracts from his diary, which he had kept in the haunted house:

"I was spending some months of the summer of '73 at a favorite watering place in the S.E. coast. One afternoon I went to visit some old friends who lived in an old house which stood in a quadrangle, and was approached from the church by a narrow lane. Brook House was a commodious, red-brick structure of three stories, faced by a Court, with its ground-floor windows unseen from the outside by reason of the lofty wall which encircled them.

"On the day in question, as I approached the house from the Church side, I happened to glance at the window to the right on the second floor. There I saw, to my astonishment, the apparent figure of Miss B., standing partially dressed, arranging her hair and looking intently at me. On entering the house, I was at once shown into the drawing-room, and I found Miss B. reading. In reply to my question, she told me she had been there an hour!

"My curiosity was now fully aroused, and I went to the house the next day, July 4, accompanied by a lady, a mutual friend. We went up into the room in which I had seen the figure, threw the window open—it being very hot—looking on to the garden, and then went downstairs into the drawing-room, where we had some music. We went up again in about half an hour's time. The window was *shut*.... We went back into the garden, and looked up at the window. Presently, to our horror, a figure appeared resembling Miss B., yet most unlike her—its fearful eyes were gazing at me without movement and totally expressionless. What, then, caused the arresting of the heart's pulsation (as it felt) and blood—that the moment before had burnt as it coursed madly through the veins—to be chilled to ice? This—one was face to face with a spirit, and withered by the contact. Those eyes—I can see them—I can feel them—after a lapse of nearly twenty years. Miss B. had incontinently fainted when she saw the shoulders (as she described it) of the figure. I continued gazing spellbound; like the 'Wedding Guest' I was held by the spirit's eye, and I could not choose but look. The dreadful hands were lifted automatically; they rested on the window sash. It came partly down, stayed a moment, then noiselessly closed, and I saw a hand rise and clasp it. I gazed steadfastly throughout. What impressed me strangely was this peculiarity, that as soon as the sash had passed the face the latter vanished, the hands remained; the unreality of the actual movement of the window, as it descended, also seemed to contradict me: it suggested (for want of a better comparison) the mechanical passage of stage scenery, and some sorts of toys that are pulled by wires; it made no noise whatever. Now I distinctly recognized the shape as that of Rhoda, Miss B.'s elder sister, who had been dead some twelve years.... We looked again, and saw the backs of two hands on the *outside* of the window, but they did not move it.

"We then went in, coming out again almost directly, and saw the window nearly closed; then went upstairs into the room; and again I flung the window as wide open as it would go, and before leaving set the door open, with a heavy chair against it; but previous to this (I omitted to mention) as we were looking up at the window after the appearance of the hands, we saw a horrible object come from the right (the apparition invariably did); it resembled a large, white bundle, called by Miss B., who had before seen it, 'The Headless Woman'; it came in front of the window and then began walking backwards and forwards. After a lapse of half an hour, we went upstairs again, and found the chair by the window, and the door closed; whereupon I wrote 'It' a letter to this effect: 'Miss B. and Mr. H. present their compliments to the "Lady Headless" and request her acceptance of this fruit from their garden; they hope it will please, as she has often been seen admiring it. A reply will oblige, but the bearer does not wait for the answer.' We put the chair once more against the window, placing the fruit and note on it; two or three times we went up, but nothing had changed.

"We then went and stood outside the summer house, whence a clear view of the window could be obtained; presently there came forward the headless figure; and distinctly bowed two or three times, then immediately afterwards a deafening slam of the door. The apex of this figure, which was rotund, *i.e.*, headless, once or twice dilated, and we feared seeing something, we knew not what; it then vanished, and we saw a beautiful arm come from the curtain and wave to us. Upstairs again, the door was shut; on entering we saw the chair overturned in the middle of the room, the fruit scattered in all directions, and, to our horror, the note, which I had folded crosswise, was charred at each corner. I took it up; but lacked the courage to open, and perhaps find a possible reply. Placing it in a plate I burnt it. The process was a very slow one; and it distilled a dark mucus.

"The whimsical idea now possessed me to arrange the room like a theatre, the armchair and others I placed facing the stand; on them I laid antimacassars, and books for programmes. We then went down to the end of the garden which commanded a view of the room, and looked: blank space, nothing more—stay! A curious filmy vapor begins to float in the air, which slowly cohered, evolved vague phantasms; they unite, and gradually assume a definite shape. The headless woman fronts us at the window, she vanishes, and an immense sheet is waved twice or thrice from the right side of the window, something is flung out; we walk quickly up the garden and there, under the window, lies one of the books. What had hastened our steps was the frantic gesticulating of the servant. She was frightened out of her senses by the peculiar sounds proceeding from the room; but she could not describe them, saying that they seemed to be a terrible hurrying to and fro, accompanied by strange noises.... We took the Bible and entered the room, which was in disorder: the flower-stand was thrown down, the two chairs widely apart, one of the antimacassars was tightly folded up under the recumbent towel horse, the other with the towel was airing itself on the gigantic tree some seven feet from the window....

"The next day we went into the room, and discovered an impression in the bed, as though some 'thing' had lain in it. On closer inspection, we distinctly saw the coverlet gently moving, resembling the very gentle respiration of a body beneath. We returned to the garden, having thrown open the window. After waiting for a long time, we saw what looked like a hand appear on the center of the window sill, then from the curtain came the white figure.

"It disappeared and after a moment or two the hand also; but there must have been a *something* besides crouching under the window, for it heaved upwards and seemed to fill the window for an instant. It then sank, the hand vanished, and we saw no more. We waited a long time, till I spoke of going. I had noticed as a curious thing that almost always, when I had wearied of looking, seeing *nothing* and about to leave, something was sure to happen....

"This ends my personal experiences. My health became impaired, and for upwards of two years I was invalided, but as time wore on and the impressions waned, I gradually recovered. I often wander back in imagination to the many mysteries that in the long ago held sway at Brook House."

CHAPTER V

GHOST STORIES OF A MORE DRAMATIC NATURE

IN the cases which are adduced in the present chapter, the standard of evidence cannot be considered so high; many of them have been recorded in good faith as actual experiences, but they will probably fail to carry conviction to the same extent as those which have gone before. Still, many of these narratives are singularly striking and interesting; and for this reason deserve to be included in this volume. The reader may therefore place any construction he may choose upon these cases; as they are presented not as evidence but as entertainment. I shall begin with some personal experiences of a Scotch seer, who, according to his own accounts, has experienced some of the most dramatic and remarkable manifestations conceivable.

DISEASE-PHANTOMS

Mr. Elliott O'Donnell—a man about whom it has

been said that "the gates of his soul are open on the Hell side," has had many strange experiences with spirits, mostly evil and horrible, and has recorded these in his books "Ghostly Phenomena," "Byways of Ghostland," etc. From his voluminous writings on his own personal experiences, I cite a few cases, to show the character of the phenomena:

"I have, from time to time, witnessed many manifestations which I believe to be super-physical, both from the peculiarity of their properties, and from the effect their presence invariably produce on me—an effect I cannot associate with anything physical. One of the first occult phenomena I remember, appeared to me when I was about five years of age. I was then living in a town in the West of England, and had, according to the usual custom, been put to bed at six o'clock. I had spent a very happy day, playing with my favorite toys—soldiers—and, not being in the least degree tired, was amusing myself with planning a fresh campaign for the following morning, when I noticed suddenly that the bedroom door (which I distinctly remember my nurse carefully latching) was slowly opening. Thinking this was very curious, but without the slightest suspicion of 'ghosts,' I sat up in bed and watched.

"The door continued to open, and at last I caught sight of something so extraordinary that my guilty conscience at once associated it with the Devil—with regard to whom I distinctly recollected to have spoken that afternoon in a sceptical, and I frankly admit, very disrespectful manner. But far from feeling the proximity of that heat which all those who profess authority on Satanic matters ascribe to Satan, I felt decidedly cold—so cold, indeed, that my hands grew numb and my teeth chattered. At first I only saw two light glittering eyes that fixed themselves upon me with an expression of diabolical glee, but I was soon able to perceive that they were set in a huge, flat face, coveredwith fulsome-looking yellow spots about the size of a threepenny bit. I do not remember noticing any of the other features, save the mouth, which was large and gaping. The body to which the head was attached was quite nude, and covered all over with spots similar to those on the face. I cannot recall any arms, though I have vivid recollections of two thick and, to all appearances, jointless legs, by the use of which it left the doorway, and gliding noiselessly over the carpet, approached the empty bed, placed in a parallel position to my own. There it halted, and thrusting its mis-shapen head forward, it fixed its malevolent eyes on me with a penetrating stare. On this occasion, I was far less frightened than on any of my subsequent experiences with the occult. Why, I cannot say, as the manifestation was certainly one of the most hideous I have ever seen. My curiosity, however, was far greater than my fear, and I kept asking myself what the thing was, and why it was there?

"It did not seem to be composed of ordinary flesh and blood, but rather of some luminous matter that resembles the light emanating from a glow-worm.

"After remaining in the same attitude for what seemed to me an incalculably long time, it gradually receded, and assuming all of a sudden a horizontal attitude, passed head first through the wall opposite to where I sat. Next day, I made a sketch of the apparition, and showed it to my relatives, who, of course, told me I had been dreaming. About two weeks later I was ill in bed with a painful, if not actually dangerous, disease. I was giving an account of this manifestation at a lecture I delivered two or three years ago in B., and when I had finished speaking, I was called aside by one of the audience who very shyly told me that he too had had a similar experience. Prior to being attacked by diphtheria, he had seen a queer-looking apparition which had approached his bedside and leaned over him. He assured me that he had been fully awake at the time, and had applied tests to prove that the phantom was entirely objective.

"A number of other cases, too, have been reported to me, in which various species of phantasms have been seen before various illnesses. Hence I believe that certain spirits are symbolical of certain diseases, if not the actual creators of the bacilli from which these diseases arise. To these phantasms I have given the name of *Morbas*...."

THE TALE OF THE MUMMY

"During one of my sojourns in Paris," says Mr. Elliott O'Donnell, in his "Byways of Ghost Land," "I met a Frenchman who, he informed me, had just returned from the East. I asked him if he had brought back any curios such as vases, funeral urns, weapons or amulets. 'Yes, lots,' he replied, 'two cases full. But no mummies! Mon Dieu! No mummies. You ask me why? Ah! Thereby hangs a tale. If you will have patience, I will tell it you.'

"The following is the gist of his narrative:

"'Some seasons ago I traveled up the Nile as far as Assiut, and when there, managed to pay a visit to the grand ruins of Thebes. Among the various treasures I brought away with me was a mummy. I found it lying in an enormous lidless sarcophagus, close to a mutilated statue of Anubis. On my return to Assiut, I had the mummy placed in my tent, and thought no more of it till something awoke me with startling suddenness in the night. Then, obeying a peculiar impulse, I turned over on my side and looked in the direction of my treasure.

"'The nights in the Soudan at this time of year are brilliant, one can even see to read, and every object in the desert is almost as clearly visible as by day. But I was quite startled by the whiteness of the glow which rested on the mummy, the face of which was immediately opposite mine. The remains—those of Met-Om-Karema, lady of the College of the god Amen-ra—were swathed in bandages, some of which had worn away in parts or become loose; and the figure, plainly discernible, was that of a shapely woman with elegant bust, well-formed limbs, rounded arms and small hands. The thumbs were slender, and the fingers, each of which was separately bandaged, long and tapering. The neck was full, the cranium rather long, the nose aquiline, the chin firm. Imitation eyes, brows, and lips were painted on the wrappings, and the effect thus produced and in the phosphorescent glare of the moonbeams, was very weird. I was quite alone in the tent, the only European who accompanied me to Assiut, having stayed in the town by preference, and my servants being encamped at one hundred or so yards from me on the ground.

"'Sound travels far in the desert, but the silence now was absolute, and, though I listened attentively, I could not detect the slightest noise—man, beast and insect were abnormally still. There was something in the air, too, which struck me as unusual; an odd, clammy coldness that reminded me at once of the catacombs in Paris. I had hardly, however, conceived the resemblance, when a sob—low, gentle, but very distinct—sent a thrill of horror through me. It was ridiculous, absurd. It could not be, and I fought against the idea as to whence the sound had proceeded, as something too utterly fantastic, too utterly impossible. I tried to occupy my mind with other thoughts—the frivolities of Cairo, the casinos of Nice; but all to no purpose; and soon, on my eager, throbbing ear there again fell that sound, that low and gentle sob. My hair stood on end; this time there was no doubt, no possible manner of doubt—the mummy lived! I looked at it aghast. I strained my vision to detect any movement in its limbs, but none was perceptible. Yet the noise had come from it, it had breathed—breathed—and even as I hissed the word unconsciously through my clenched lips, the bosom of the mummy rose and fell.

"'A frightful terror seized me. I tried to shriek to

my servants; I could not ejaculate a syllable. I tried to close my eye-lids, but they were held open as in a vice. Again there came a sob that was immediately succeeded by a sigh; and a tremor ran through the figure from head to foot. One of its hands then began to move, the fingers clutched the air convulsively, then grew rigid, then curled slowly into the palms, then suddenly straightened. The bandages concealing them from view then fell off, and to my agonized sight were disclosed objects that struck me as strangely familiar. There is something about fingers, a marked individuality, I never forget. No two persons' hands are alike. And in these fingers, in their excessive whiteness, round knuckles, and blue veins, I read a likeness whose prototype, struggle how I would, I could not recall. Gradually the hand moved upwards, and, reaching the throat, the fingers set to work at once to remove the wrappings. My terror was now sublime. I dare not imagine, I dare not for one instant think, what I should see. And there was no getting away from it; I could not stir an inch, and the ghastly revelation would take place within a yard of my face!

"'One by one the bandages came off. A glimmer of skin, pale as marble; the beginning of the nose, the whole nose; the upper lip, exquisitely, delicately cut; the teeth, white and even on the whole, but here and there a shining gold filling; the under lip, soft and gentle; a mouth I knew, but—God, where? In my dreams, in the wild fantasies that had oft-times visited by pillow at night—in delirium, in reality, where? Mon Dieu! WHERE?

"'The uncasing continued. The chin next, a chin that was purely feminine, purely classical; then the upper part of the head—the hair long, black, luxuriant—the forehead low and white—the brows black, firmly pencilled; and last of all, the eyes!—and as they met my frenzied gaze, smiled, smiled right down into the depths of my living soul, I recognized them—they were the eyes of my mother, my mother who had died in my boyhood! Seized with a madness that knew no bounds, I sprang to my feet. The figure rose and confronted me. I flung open my arms to embrace her, the woman of all women in the world I loved best, the only woman I had ever loved. Shrinking from my touch, she cowered against the side of the tent. I fell on my knees before her and kissed—what? Not the feet of my mother, but those of the long-buried dead. Sick with repulsion and fear I looked up, and there bending over and peering into my eyes was the face, the fleshless, mouldering face of the foul and barely recognizable corpse! With a shriek of horror I rolled backwards, and, springing to my feet, prepared to fly. I glanced at the mummy. It was lying on the ground, stiff and still, every bandage in its place; whilst standing over it, a look of fiendish glee in its light, doglike eyes, was the figure of Anubis, lurid and menacing.

"'The voices of my servants, assuring me they were coming, broke the silence, and in an instant the apparition vanished.

"'I had had enough of the tent, however, at least for that night, and, seeking refuge in the town, I whiled away the hours till morning with a fragrant cigar and a novel. Directly I had breakfasted, I took the mummy back to Thebes, and left it there. No thank you, Mr. O'Donnell, I collect many kinds of curios, but—no more mummies!'"

FACE SLAPPED BY A GHOST

The following remarkable event occurred to a friend of mine—an elderly, married lady, whom I have known for some time. She is now making her home in Brooklyn, but at the time of her gruesome experience was residing in England. It is some years since this occurred, but the incident, she assured me, lives just as vividly in her mind as though it all happened yesterday. This is her story, just as she told it to me:

"I was staying with some friends in the country. They had an old, rambling house, with long, draughty halls and corridors all over it. As the house was already full of guests, I had to sleep in a large room, at the end of the long passage, on the ground floor. The room in itself was comfortable enough—large and warm. Yet there was an atmosphere about that apartment which I did not quite like; in fact, the whole house made me feel 'creepy,' for no reason that I can give.

"Bed-time came all too soon; and I took my candle and was shown my room. My hostess saw that I had everything I needed; and then, saying good-night, went upstairs to bed.

"I had half undressed when I saw the door of my room gently and quietly opened, as though a stealthy hand were softly pressing it open. I gazed transfixed, until, when wide open, I could see that no one was, in reality, on the other side of the door. At that I drew a breath of relief. 'A draught,' I thought, 'coming down the hallway. It is nothing.' And I chided myself on my fears; shut the door, and proceeded to undress.

"I had not gone far, however, when to my amazement the door opened again; just as quietly and stealthily as before. Again I closed the door, and proceeded with my undressing. I had by this time finished, and had donned my night-gown preparatory to getting into bed.

"At that moment I was horrified to see my door open for the *third* time, just as it did before—slowly, slowly, until it rested on its hinges, wide open to the hall. I now determined to investigate; so, taking my candle in my hand, I stepped out into the hall and proceeded down towards the front door.

"I had not taken more than three or four steps, however, when the candle in my hands was extinguished—as though a breath of wind, coming from nowhere, had blown it out. I did not much relish this, as the matches were in my room. But I determined to keep on, in the dark, and see what the cause of this could be. So I kept on and on, down the dark hall—my left hand holding the extinguished candle; my right extended so that I could feel the solid masonry all the way down the corridor.

"I had proceeded, perhaps, half way, when a strange thing occurred. I suddenly felt myself slapped on the left cheek by something cold and moist and clammy. I put my hand up to my face, and felt it was wet. For an instant I hesitated; then I proceeded, down the hall, until I came to the front door. That I found closed and locked. Having thus explored the whole length of the hall and found nothing, I turned back to regain my room. Still holding the candle in my left hand, and still feeling the wall with my outstretched right hand, I crept cautiously along, not knowing what to expect.

"Again, I had proceeded about half way down the hall when I felt the same cold, quick slap in the face (this time on the right cheek) and again I found it was wet.

"Thoroughly frightened now, I fled to my room as fast as my legs could carry me. Once within, I closed and secured the door by placing a chair against it. Next, finding my box of matches, I relighted my candle. Then I surveyed myself in the mirror, to see what could be upon my face.

"Imagine my horror when, on looking in the glass, I discovered two long streaks of blood, one upon either cheek! I was so terror-struck that I gazed at myself for a few moments unable to move or speak. Then I screamed, and after that I have no very clear recollection of what happened. I have a hazy recollection of anxious faces bending over me; of a low hum of voices; then oblivion.

"It took me many weeks to recover from the shock of that night."

ALONE WITH A GHOST IN A CHURCH

The following case is sent me by a correspondent:

I once knew a young man by the name of Charles D. Bradlaugh, who took a delight in ridiculing ghost stories and, whenever possible, in proving them to be due to fraud, trickery or hallucination. He stated he was "afraid of nothing." I said to him one day in conversation: "If you are as fearless as you say, would you be willing to spend a night alone, locked up in a Church with a corpse freshly placed in its coffin?"

He replied that he would do it any time; so the test was shortly arranged. One of the parishioners had just died, and had been placed in the crypt of the church, with the lid of the coffin removed. The lights were all extinguished; we locked the door after us, and went away, leaving Bradlaugh and the spirits to fight it out between them.

What occurred during the night must be told in Bradlaugh's own words, as nearly as I can recall them:

"When I heard the key turn in the door, that night, I confess that a strange feeling came over me for the first time in my life. I wanted to get out; but of course I knew it was useless; and in the next place my pride forbade my leaving. Shaking off the superstitious fear that had settled upon me, I turned away; and proceeded to explore, as best I could, the whole of the church.

"A bright moonlight fell in through the windows, casting queer shadows in various directions; and across the long rows of pews and the altar at the far end of the church. I walked about, looking at everything curiously, as it had been long since I found myself inside a church. Then I proceeded to the crypt, and, walking boldly up to the coffin, I gazed long and earnestly at the corpse lying within it, as though to familiarize myself with it. I went on the principle that 'familiarity breeds contempt.' When I had done this, I went back to the nave of the church, and, finding a comfortable place, I lay down, and was soon in a state bordering on sleep. I should have been asleep, probably, very soon; but, just as I was dropping off, I heard a faint sound coming from the direction of the crypt. It was like a deep sigh, and this was followed by other sounds which I find it hard to describe. All I know is that, in the quiet and stillness of that awful place, those sounds, slight as they were, were truly appalling, and chilled the very blood in my veins. Their very indistinctness added to their terror. I could not conceive what could make such uncanny noises. I sat up, and strained my eyes in the darkness, trying to penetrate the gloom. Then I heard the first faint footsteps coming up the stairs from the crypt! At first, these were faint, but they became louder and louder; until finally I could hear them plainly. Undoubtedly they were foot-falls, as though a human being were mounting the steps from the crypt where the corpse had been laid!

"I rose from my seat, my hair standing on end, while queer, cold shivers ran up and down my back. I advanced one or two paces toward the door, hardly knowing what to expect. Then, as I looked, I saw step into the bright moonlight, the corpse that a few moments before I had seen lying in the coffin downstairs!

"Frantic with fear, I rushed at the corpse, still shrouded, as it was, in the white wrappings which, torn and dishevelled, still enveloped the body. I raised one hand as though to strike the ghost, and thrust the hateful thing from me; when I felt a stunning blow on the point of my jaw, and a moment later I had lost sensibility. When I awoke, you were all round me. You know the rest."

To make a long story short, it turned out that the supposed "corpse" was not really dead at all, but in a sort of trance; and had been buried prematurely. He had revived in the night; and was advancing into the church when he encountered Bradlaugh in the doorway. Thinking him a robber or an assassin, he had struck first; and, being a powerful man and a good boxer, he had knocked out Bradlaugh by a blow on the jaw. When we arrived in the morning, we found Bradlaugh senseless, and the "corpse," now stripped of his grave clothes, bending over him, dashing cold water in his face!

A HAUNTED HOUSE IN FRANCE

The following case, said to be authentic, is quoted here because of the incident of the "shouts and laughter" which were heard, and which serve to throw an interesting sidelight on the case which follows it.

The Rev. F. G. Lee, in his book, *Sights and Shadows*,

gives the following account, sent to him, of a haunted house in France:

"In the spring of the year 1891, great excitement was occasioned by a disembodied spirit in a haunted house in LePort, at Nice. This is situated in a terrace close to the quarries, where, after the reports concerning it, as many as two thousand persons were often gathered round it. The spirits haunting it—never visible, however—would beat the inmates so unmercifully that the blows would leave bruises. Hundreds of persons saw the result, and testified to the undoubted facts. The local police, on being appealed to, and having heard the evidence of numerous eye-witnesses, and of those persons who were inconvenienced, formed a body of organized inquirers, who, shrewd enough in mundane matters, utterly failed to discover anything or anybody.

"On one occasion, thirteen men sat up in three rooms which had been well lighted, and some of them played cards for several hours to while away the time. During the whole of this occurrence, the strangest noises were heard in various parts of the building. It seemed, at one time, as if a whole regiment of soldiers were tramping up the chief staircase. Pictures swung to and fro upon the walls, without any visible motive effect.[4] Then heavy blows were heard on the walls, and it appeared that the closed doors and the shutters were being violently struck and thumped, as if with a large hammer wrapped in cloth.

---

[4] This is a common feature of haunted houses.—H.C.

"On two occasions, a room on the ground floor was found to be in the densest darkness, though outside the house the sun was shining. On another occasion, just before midnight, when certain persons were specially present to note any supernatural occurrences, all the lamps in the house were suddenly put out; while shouts and laughter were heard in every part of the place, more particularly from the empty rooms. At the same time, heavy blows were experienced by those present, who were very severely bruised, and a large bottle of ink was thrown by invisible hands from the top of the staircase.

"Every attempt was made to discover the source of these extraordinary disorders, but without avail. They were reported to have ceased for several months, but to have commenced again at a later period. A local communication says that they still 'occur at intervals.'"

A HAUNTED HOUSE IN GEORGIA

The following account is taken from the report of the San Francisco *Examiner*, and is certainly one of the most striking cases of the character on record. It is not put forward as strictly "evidential," but its interesting nature certainly warrants its insertion in this volume.

"Soon after the Walsinghams took up their abode in their new home, they began to be disturbed by strange sounds and odd phenomena. These disturbances generally took the form of noises in the house after the family had retired and the lights had been extinguished—continual banging of the doors, things overturned, the doorbell rang, and the annoying of the house dog, a large and intelligent mastiff.

"One day Don Cæsar, the mastiff, was found in the hallway barking furiously and bristling with rage, while his eyes seemed directed to the wall just before him. At last he made a spring forward with a hoarse yelp of ungovernable fury, only to fall back as if flung down by some powerful and cruel hand. Upon examination it was found that his neck had been broken.

"The house cat, on the contrary, seemed rather to enjoy the favor of the ghost, and would often enter a door as if escorting some visitor, whose hand was stroking her back. She would also climb about a chair, rubbing herself and purring as if well pleased at the presence of some one in the seat. She and Don Cæsar invariably manifested this eccentric conduct at the same time, as though the mysterious being were visible to both of them.

"The annoying visitant finally took to arousing the family at all hours of the night by making such a row as to render any rest impossible.

"This noise, which consisted of shouts, groans, hideous laughter, and a peculiar, most distressing wail, would sometimes proceed, apparently, from under the house, sometimes from the ceiling and at other times in the very room in which the family was seated. One night Miss Amelia Walsingham, the young lady daughter, was engaged at her toilet, when she felt a hand softly laid on her shoulder. Thinking it her mother or sister, she glanced at the glass before her, only to be thunderstruck at seeing the mirror reflect no form but her own, though she could plainly see a man's broad hand lying on her arm.

"She brought the family to her by her screams, but when they reached her all sign of the mysterious hand had gone. Mr. Walsingham himself saw footsteps form beside his own while walking through the garden after a light rain.

"The marks were those of a man's naked feet, and fell beside his own, as if the person walked at his side.

"Matters grew so serious that the Walsinghams became frightened, and talked of leaving the house, when an event took place which confirmed them in this determination. The family was seated at the supper table with several guests who were spending the evening when a loud groan was heard in the room overhead.

"This was, however, nothing unusual, and very little notice was taken of it until one of the visitors pointed out a stain of what looked like blood on the white table cloth, and it was seen that some liquid was slowly dripping on the table from the ceiling overhead. This liquid was so much like freshly-shed blood that it horrified those who watched its slow dropping. Mr. Walsingham, with several of his guests, ran hastily upstairs and into the room directly over the one in which the blood was dripping.

"A carpet covered the floor, and nothing appeared to explain the source of the ghastly rain; but, anxious to satisfy themselves thoroughly, the carpet was immediately ripped up, and the boarding found to be perfectly dry, and even covered with a thin layer of dust, and all the while the floor was being examined the persons below could swear the blood never ceased to drop. A stain the size of a dinner-plate was formed before the drops ceased to fall. This stain was examined the next day under the microscope, and was pronounced by competent chemists to be human blood.

"The Walsinghams left the house next day, and since then the place has been apparently given over to spooks and evil spirits, which make the night hideous with the noise of revel, shouts and furious yells. Hundreds from all over this county and adjacent ones have visited the place, but few have had the courage to pass the night in the haunted house. One daring spirit, however, Horace Gunn, of Savannah, accepted a wager that he could not spend twenty-four hours in it, and did so, though he declares that there is not enough money in the country to make him pass another night there. He was found the morning after by his friends with whom he made the wager, in a swoon. He has never recovered from the shock of his horrible experience, and is still confined to his bed suffering from nervous prostration.

"His story is that shortly after nightfall he endeavored to kindle a fire in one of the rooms, and to light the lamp with which he had provided himself, but to his surprise and consternation, found it impossible to do either. An icy breath, which seemed to proceed from some invisible person at his side, extinguished each match as he lighted it. At this peculiarly terrifying turn of affairs Mr. Gunn would have left the house and forfeited the amount of his wager, a considerable one, but he was restrained by the fear of ridicule. He steadied himself in the dark with what calmness he could, and waited developments.

"For some time nothing occurred, and the young man was half-dozing, when, after an hour or two, he was brought to his feet by a sudden yell of pain or rage that seemed to come from under the house. This appeared to be the signal for an outbreak of hideous noises all over the house. The sound of running feet could be heard scurrying up and down the stairs, hastening from one room to another, as if one person fled from the pursuit of a second. This kept up for nearly an hour, but at last ceased altogether, and for some time Mr. Gunn sat in darkness and quiet, and had about concluded that the performance was over for the night. At last, however, his attention was attracted by a white spot that gradually appeared on the opposite wall.

"The spot continued to brighten, until it seemed a disc of white fire, when the horrified spectator saw that the light emanated from and surrounded a human head, which, without a body, or any visible means of support, was moving slowly along the wall, about the height of a man from the floor. This ghastly head appeared to be that of an aged person, though whether male or female it was difficult to determine. The hair was long and gray, and matted together with dark clots of blood, which also issued from a deep jagged wound in one temple. The cheeks were fallen in and the whole face indicated suffering and unspeakable misery. The eyes were wide open, and gleamed with an unearthly fire, while the glassy eyes seemed to follow the terror-stricken Gunn, who was too thoroughly paralyzed by what he saw to move or cry out. Finally, the head disappeared and the room was once more left in darkness, but the young man could hear what seemed to be half a dozen persons moving about him, while the whole house shook as if rocked by some violent earthquake.

"The groaning and the wailing that broke forth from every direction was something terrific, and an unearthly rattle and banging as of china or tin pans being flung to the ground floor from the upper story added to the deafening noise. Gunn at last roused himself sufficiently to try and leave the haunted house. Feeling his way along the wall, in order to avoid the beings, whatever they were, that filled the room, the young man had nearly succeeded in reaching the door when he found himself seized by the ankle and was violently thrown to the floor. He was grasped by icy hands, which sought to grip him about the throat. He struggled with his unseen foe, but was soon overpowered and choked into insensibility. When found by his friends, his throat was black with the marks of long, thin fingers, armed with cruel, curved nails.

"The only explanation which, can be found for these mysterious manifestations is that about three months before, a number of bones were discovered on the Walsingham place, which some declared even then to be those of a human being. Mr. Walsingham pronounced them, however, to be an animal's, and they were hastily thrown into an adjacent limekiln.

It is supposed to be the outraged spirit of a person to whom they belonged in life which is now creating such consternation."

SHAKEN BY A GHOST

The following narrative is vouched for by Mrs. H. S. Iredell, of Tunbridge Wells, England, a relative of the Rev. Dr. Lee, who gives the case in his *Sights and Shadows*:

"The haunted house in question is near Wandsworth common. The late occupants of it were a man, his wife and their child. They had to leave it, for they could get no rest in it at night for the fearful noises which went on incessantly, like sounds as of a sledge-hammer wrapped in flannel struck against the walls. The sister-in-law of the late occupants, who told me of it, had spent some days at the house, so I heard all the story first-hand. One night she likewise felt as if someone had taken her by the shoulders and she was being roughly shaken from side to side. Her husband, who was with her, saw her at the time she was being shaken by an invisible power, stretched out his hand to take hold of her; but he felt right up his arm to his shoulder a *shoc*k, as it were of electricity, which made him instantly draw back and cry out. Nothing was ever seen, but in the special sleeping-room which seemed to be haunted, the clothes used to be pulled off the bed at night and thrown on the floor, and then they used to raise or rear themselves up again on the bed....

"Since the above was written, it is reported, that no less than five families have respectively occupied the house as tenants, who one and all have left it as soon as possible. It is now said to be permanently untenanted."

This case is given because of the incident of the "electric shock" which the percipient received, when attempting to interfere with the "spirit"; and serves as an interesting modern and apparently well-authenticated instance of what occurred in Lytton's story, which follows.

THE HOUSE AND THE BRAIN

Bulwer Lytton's story, "The House and the Brain," is, perhaps, the most remarkable ghost story of this character on record, and is considered, by many, the best ever written. The phenomena occur in a house which is reputed to be haunted; no one will live in it. At last one brave soul determines to pass the night within its walls; he and his servant take up their abode in it, and, after various startling adventures of a minor character, the "grand climax" of the night is reached. As the author sat reading by the fire, the following occurred, which is told in his own words:

"I now became aware that something interposed between the page and the light—the page was over-shadowed; I looked up, and I saw what I shall find it very difficult, perhaps impossible, to describe.

"It was a Darkness shaping itself forth from the air in very undefined outline. I cannot say it was a human form, and yet it had more resemblance to a human form, or rather shadow, than to anything else. As it stood, wholly apart and distinct from the air and light around it, its dimensions seemed gigantic, the summit nearly touching the ceiling. While I gazed, a feeling of intense cold seized me. An iceberg could not more have chilled me; nor could the cold of an iceberg have been more purely physical. I feel convinced that it was not the cold caused by fear. As I continued to gaze, I thought—but this I cannot say with precision—that I distinguished two eyes looking on me from the height. One moment I fancied that I distinguished them clearly; the next they seemed gone; but still two rays of pale blue light frequently shot through the darkness, as from the height on which, I half believed, half doubted, that I had encountered the eyes.

"I strove to speak—my voice utterly failed me; I could only think to myself, Is this fear? It is *not* fear! I strove to rise; in vain; I felt weighed down by an irresistible force. Indeed, my impression was that of an immense and overwhelming Power opposed to my volition; that sense of utter inadequacy to cope with a force beyond man's, which one may feel *physically* in a storm at sea, in a conflagration, or when confronting some terrible wild beast—or rather, perhaps, the shark of the ocean, I felt *morally*. Opposed to my will was another will, as far superior to its strength as storm, fire and shark are superior in material force to the force of man.

"And now—as this impression grew on me—now came, at last, horror—horror of a degree that no words can convey. Still I retained pride, if not courage; and in my own mind I said: 'This is horror, but it is not fear; unless I fear I cannot be harmed; my reason rejects this thing; it is an illusion—I do not fear.' With a violent effort I succeeded at last in stretching out my hand towards the weapon on the table; as I did so, on the arm and shoulder I received a strange shock, and my arm fell to my side powerless. And now, to add to my horror, the light began slowly to wane from the candles—they were not, as it were, extinguished, but their flame seemed very gradually withdrawn—it was the same with the fire; the light was extinguished from the fuel; in a few minutes the room was in utter darkness. The dread that came over me, to be thus in the dark with that Thing, whose power was so intensely felt, brought on a reaction of nerve. In fact, terror had reached that climax, that either my senses must have deserted me, or I must have burst through the spell. I *did* burst through it. I found voice, though the voice was a shriek. I remember that I broke forth with words like these—'I do not fear, my soul does not fear'; and at the same time I found the strength to rise. Still in that profound gloom I rushed to one of the windows—tore aside the curtain—flung open the shutters; my first thought was—LIGHT. And when I saw the moon high, clear and calm, I felt a joy that almost compensated me for my previous terror. There was the moon; there also was the light from the gas lamps in the deserted, slumberous street. I turned to look back into the room; the moon penetrated its shadow very palely and partially—but still there was light. The dark Thing, whatever it might be, was gone—except that I could yet see a dim shadow, which seemed the shadow of that shade against the opposite wall.

"My eye now rested on the table, and from under the table (which was without cloth or cover—an old mahogany round table) there rose a hand, visible as far as the wrist. It was a hand, seemingly, as much of flesh and blood as my own, but the hand of an aged person—lean, wrinkled, small too—a woman's hand. That hand very softly closed on the two letters that lay on the table; hand and letters both vanished. Then there came the same three loud, measured knocks I had heard on the bed-head before this extraordinary drama commenced.

"As these sounds slowly ceased, I felt the whole room vibrate sensibly; and at the far end there rose, from the floor, sparks or globules, like globules of light, many colored—green, yellow, fire-red, azure. Up and down, to and fro, hither, thither, as tiny Will o' the Wisps, the sparks moved, slow and swift, each at its own caprice. A chair (as in the drawing-room below) was now advanced from the wall without apparent agency, and placed at the opposite side of the table. Suddenly, as forth from the air, there grew a shape, a woman's shape. It was distinct as a shape of life—ghastly as the shape of death. The face was that of youth, with a strange, mournful beauty; the throat and shoulders were bare; the rest of the form in a loose robe of cloudy white. It began sleeking its long, yellow hair, which fell over its shoulders; its eyes were not turned towards me, but to the floor; it seemed listening, watching, waiting. The shadow of the shade in the background grew darker; and again I thought I saw the eyes gleaming out from the summit of the shadow—eyes fixed upon that shape.

"As if from the door, though it did not open, there grew out another shape, equally distinct, equally ghastly—a man's shape—a young man's. It was in the dress of the last century, or rather the likeness to such dress (for both the male and the female, though defined, were evidently unsubstantial, impalpable, simulacra, phantasms), and there was something incongruous, grotesque, yet fearful in the contrast between the elaborate finery, the courtly precision of that old-fashioned garb, with its ruffles and lace and buckles, and the corpse-like aspect and ghost-like stillness of the flitting wearer. Just as the male shape approached the female, the dark shadow started from the wall, and all three for a moment were wrapped in darkness. When the pale light returned, the two phantasms were as if in the grasp of the shadow, that towered between them, and there was a blood stain on the breast of the female; and the phantom male was leaning on its phantom sword, and blood seemed trickling fast from the ruffles, from the lace; and the darkness of the intermediate Shadow swallowed them up—they were gone. And again the bubbles of light shot, and sailed, and undulated, growing thicker and thicker and more wildly confused in their movements.

"The closet door to the right of the fireplace now opened, and from the aperture there came the form of an aged woman. In her hand she held letters—the very letters over which I had seen the hand close; and behind her I heard a footstep. She turned round as if to listen, and then she opened her letters and seemed to read; and over her shoulder I saw a livid face, the face of a man long drowned—bloated, bleached—seaweed tangled in its dripping hair, and at her feet lay a form as of a corpse, and beside the corpse there towered a child, a miserable, squalid child, with famine in its cheeks and fear in its eyes. And as I looked in the old woman's face, the wrinkles and lines vanished; and it became the face of youth—hard-eyed, stony, but still youth; and the Shadow darted forth and darkened over these phantoms as it had darkened over the last.

"Nothing now was left but the Shadow, and on that my eyes were intently fixed, till again eyes grew out of the Shadow—malignant, serpent eyes. And the bubbles of light again rose and fell, and in their disordered, irregular, turbulent maze, mingled with the wan moonlight. And now from these globules themselves, as from the shell of an egg, monstrous things burst out; the air grew filled with them; larvæ so bloodless and so hideous that I can in no way describe them except to remind the reader of the swarming life which the solar microscope brings before the eyes in a drop of water—things transparent, supple, agile, chasing each other, devouring each other—forms like nought ever beheld by the naked eye. As the shapes were without symmetry, so their movements were without order. In their very vagrancies there was no sport; they came round me and round; thicker and faster and swifter, swarming over my head, crawling over my right arm, which was outstretched in involuntary command against all evil things. Sometimes I felt myself touched, but not by them; invisible hands touched me. Once I felt the clutch of cold, soft fingers at my throat, I was still equally conscious that if I gave way to fear I should be in bodily peril; and I concentrated all my faculties in the single focus of resisting, stubborn will. And I turned my sight from the Shadow—above all, from those strange serpent eyes—eyes that had now become distinctly visible. For there, though in nought else round me, I was aware that there was a WILL, and a will of intense, creative, working evil, which might crush down my own.

"The pale atmosphere in the room began now to redden as if in the air of some near conflagration. The larvæ grew lurid as things that live on fire. Again the room vibrated; again I heard the three measured knocks; and again all things were swallowed up in the darkness of the dark shadow—as if out of that darkness all had come, into that darkness all had returned.

"As the gloom receded, the Shadow was wholly gone. Slowly, as it had been withdrawn, the flame grew again into the candles on the table, again into the fuel in the grate....

"The room came once more calmly, healthfully into sight.

"Nothing more chanced for the rest of the night. Nor, indeed, had I long to wait before the dawn broke...."

APPENDIX A

HISTORICAL GHOSTS

Royalty and well-known personages have seen ghosts in all ages of the world's history; certainly they are not exempt from the common run of humanity so far as ghostly visitations are concerned! Mr. Stead has compiled a number of notable cases of this character, of which the following are probably the most noteworthy:

ROYAL

Henry IV. of France told D'Aubigne that, in the presence of himself, the Archbishop of Lyons, and three ladies of the Court, the Queen (Margaret of Valois) saw the apparition of a certain Cardinal afterwards found to have died at the moment.

Abel the Fratricide, King of Denmark, still haunts the woods of Poole, near the city of Sleswig.

Valdemar IV. haunts Gurre Wood, near Elsinore.

Charles XI., of Sweden, accompanied by his chamberlain and state physician, witnessed the trial of the assassin of Gartavus III., which occurred nearly a century later.

James IV., of Scotland, was warned by an apparition against his intended expedition into England. He, however, proceeded and fell at Flodden Field.

Charles I., of England, was also warned by an apparition, but paying no heed, was disastrously defeated at Naseby.

Queen Elizabeth is said to have been warned of her death by the apparition of her own double.

EMPERORS

Trajan and *Caracalla* both saw apparitions, which they recorded.

Theodosius and *Julian the Apostate* both beheld apparitions, at important crises in their lives.

FAMOUS MEN

Sir Robert Peel and his brother both saw Lord Byron in London when he was in reality lying dangerously ill of a fever in Patras. During the same fever, he also appeared to others.

Julius Caesar, Xerxes, Drusus, Pausanius, Dio (General of Syracuse), *Admiral Coligni* all saw apparitions, which made a deep impression on them in every case.

Napoleon, at St. Helena, saw and conversed with the apparition of Josephine, who warned him of his approaching death. *Blucher*, on the day of his death, was also told of it by an apparition. *General Garfield* saw and conversed with his father, latterly deceased. *Lincoln* had a certain premonitory dream which occurred three times in relation to important battles, and the fourth on the eve of his assassination.

Dante, son of the poet, was visited in a dream by his father, who conversed with him and told him (correctly) where to find the missing thirteen cantos of the "Commedia."

Goethe saw his own double riding by his side under conditions which really occurred years later.

Tasso saw and conversed with beings invisible to those about him.

Cellini was dissuaded from suicide by the apparition of a young man who frequently visited and encouraged him.

Mozart was visited by a mysterious person who ordered him to compose a *requiem*, and came frequently to inquire after its progress, but disappeared on its completion, which occurred just in time for its performance at his own funeral.

Ben Johnson was visited by the apparition of his eldest son with the mark of a bloody cross upon his forehead at the moment of his death by the plague.

Thackery wrote: "It is all very well for you who have probably never seen spirit manifestations to talk as you do, but had you seen what I have witnessed you would hold a different opinion."

Hugh Miller, Maria Edgeworth, Captain Marryat, Madame de Stael, Sir Humphrey Davy, William Harvey, Francis

— TRUE GHOST STORIES —

Bacon, Martin Luther, George Fox, Cardinal Newman, Bishop Wilberforce, and many others have seen apparitions, or held converse with the unseen world in one form or another, as recorded by themselves.

Among the famous historical hauntings, we must not forget to mention the famous *Cock Lane Ghost* which occurred about 1760. According to a brief paragraph printed in the *London Ledger*, 1762, we read that:

"For some time a great knocking having been heard in the night, at the officiating parish clerk's of St. Sepulchre's, in Cock Lane near Smithfield, to the great terror of the family, and all means used to discover the meaning of it having failed, four gentlemen sat up there last Friday night, among whom was a clergyman standing withinside the door, who asked various questions. On his asking whether anyone had been murdered, no answer was made; but on his asking whether anyone had been poisoned, it knocked one and thirty times. The report current in the neighborhood is that a woman was some time ago poisoned, and buried in St. John's Clerkenwell, by her brother-in-law."

These knockings and phenomena occurred for a considerable time, until the whole community became interested in the manifestations. While various theories were advanced at the time—and since—to explain this ghost, no definite conclusion has ever been arrived at.

The *Drummer of Tedworth* is a still older and equally famous ghost, who flourished about a hundred years before the Cock Lane Ghost, and was investigated (and the results carefully recorded) by Sir Joseph Glanvil, F.R.S., who wrote a book about the case: "*Sadducismus Triumphatus*," which was also devoted to the general phenomena of witchcraft. Here, also, we find records of unaccountable "knockings" and similar phenomena, which lasted for a considerable time, and which have never yet been explained.

The ghost which invaded *John Wesley's* house stayed with them for several years, and manifested his presence in a variety of elaborate and ingenious ways. Those who are interested in this ghost and his doings should read Wesley's *Journal*; also the various discussions, *pro* and *con.*, which have appeared in the *Proceedings* of the Society for Psychical Research, from time to time. It is a most curious and suggestive record.

The *Devils of Loudon* might also be cited as an interesting case of psychic phenomena; and here trance, automatic speech, etc., were observed—as well as the usual physical phenomena. This is perhaps one of the earliest cases which was closely observed, and in which skeptical criticism was applied. This case will be found recorded in Mr. H. Addington Bruce's "*Historic Ghosts and Ghost Hunters.*"

APPENDIX B

THE PHANTOM ARMIES SEEN IN FRANCE

History abounds in cases showing the apparent intrusion of spiritual help in time of trouble, and in the annals of military history, these accounts are not lacking. On several occasions, the Crusaders thought that they saw angelic hosts fighting for them—phantom horsemen charging the enemy, when their own utter destruction seemed imminent. In the wars between the English and the Scotch, several such cases were cited, and the Napoleonic wars also furnished examples. But the most striking evidence of this character—because the newest—and supported, apparently, by a good deal of first-hand and sincere testimony, is that afforded by the Phantom Armies seen in France during the retreat of the British army from Mons—the field of Agincourt. Cut off by overwhelming numbers, and all but annihilated, the British army fought desperately, but the 80,000 were opposed by 300,000 Germans, backed by a terrific fire of artillery, and were indeed in a critical position. They were only saved, as we know, by the heroism of a small force of men—a rearguard—who were practically wiped out in consequence. At the most critical moment came what appeared to be angelic assistance. The tide of battle seemed to be stemmed by supernatural means. In a letter written by a soldier who actually witnessed these startling events, quoted by the Hon. Mrs. St. John Mildmay (*North American Review*, August, 1915), the following graphic account is given. Our soldier writes—

"The men joked at the shells and found many funny names for them, and had bets about them, and greeted them with music-hall songs, as they screamed in this terrific cannonade.... The climax seemed to have been reached, but 'a seven-times heated hell' of the enemy's onslaught fell upon them, rending brother from brother. At that very moment, they saw from their trenches a tremendous host moving against their lines. Five hundred of the thousand (who had been detailed to fight the rearguard action) remained, and as far as they could see the German infantry was pressing on against them, column by column, a grey world of men—10,000 of them, as it appeared afterwards. There was no hope at all. Some of them shook hands. One man improvised a new version of the battle song Tipperary, ending 'and we shan't get there!' And all went on firing steadily.... The enemy dropped line after line, while the few machine guns did their best. Everyone knew it was of no use. The dead grey bodies lay in companies and battalions, but others came on and on, swarming and advancing from beyond and beyond.

"'World without end, Amen,' said one of the British soldiers, with some irreverence, as he took aim and fired. Then he remembered a vegetarian restaurant in London, where he had once or twice eaten queer dishes of cutlets made of lentils and nuts that pretended to be steaks. On all the plates in this restaurant a figure of St. George was printed in blue with the motto, *Adsit Anglis Sanctus Georgius* (May St. George be a present help to England!) The soldier happened to know 'Latin and other useless things,' so now, as he fired at the grey advancing mass, 300 yards away, he uttered the pious vegetarian motto. He went on firing to the end, till at last Bill on his right had to clout him cheerfully on the head to make him stop, pointing out as he did so that the King's ammunition cost money and was not lightly to be wasted.... For, as the Latin scholar uttered his invocation, he felt something between a shudder and an electric shock pass through his body. The roar of the battle died down in his ears to a gentle murmur, and instead of it, he says, he heard a great voice louder than a thunder peal, crying 'Array! Array!' His heart grew hot as a burning coal, then it grew cold as ice within him, for it seemed to him a tumult of voices answered to the summons. He heard or seemed to hear thousands shouting:

> "'*St. George! St. George!*
> "'*Ha! Messire, Ha! Sweet Saint, grant us good deliverance!*

"'*St. George for Merrie England!*
"'*Harow! Harow! Monseigneur St. George, succour us, Ha! St. George! A low bow, and a strong bow, Knight of Heaven, aid us!*'

"As the soldier heard these voices, he saw before him, beyond the trench, a long line of shapes with a shining about them. They were like men who drew the bow, and with another shout their cloud of arrows flew singing through the air toward the German host. The other men in the trenches were firing all the while. They had no hope, but they aimed just as if they had been shooting at Bisley.

"Suddenly one of these lifted up his voice in plain English. 'Gawd help us,' he bellowed to the man next him, 'but we're bloomin' marvels! Look at those grey gentlemen! Look at them! They're not going down in dozens or hundreds—its *thousands* it is! Look, look! There's a regiment gone while I'm talking to ye!'

"'Shut it,' the other soldier bellowed, taking aim. 'What are ye talkin' about?' But he gulped with astonishment even as he spoke, for indeed the grey men were falling by the thousands. The English could hear the guttural scream of their revolvers as they shot, and line after line crashed to the earth. All the while the Latin-bred soldier heard the cry 'Harow, Harow! Monseigneur! Dear Saint! Quick to our aid! St. George help us!'

"The singing arrows darkened the air, the hordes melted before them. 'More machine guns,' Bill yelled to Tom. 'Don't hear them,' Tom yelled back, 'but thank God, anyway, that they have got it in the neck!'

"In fact, there were ten thousand dead German soldiers left before that salient of the English army, and consequently—*no Sedan*. In Germany the General Staff decided that the English must have employed turpenite shells, as no wounds were discernible on the bodies of the dead soldiers. But the man who knew what nuts tasted like when they called themselves steak, knew also that St. George had brought his Agincourt Bowmen to help the English."

Such accounts have been confirmed by others. Thus, Miss Phyllis Campbell, writing in "*The Occult Review*" (October, 1915), says:

"I tremble, now that it is safely past, to look back on the terrible week that brought the Allies to Vitry-le-Francois. We had not had our clothes off for the whole of that week, because no sooner had we reached home, too weary to undress, or to eat, and fallen on our beds, than the 'chug-chug' of the commandant's car would sound into the silence of the deserted street, and the horn would imperatively summon us back to duty—because, in addition to our duties as *ambulancier auxiliare*, we were interpreters to the post, now at this moment diminished to half-a-dozen.

"Returning at 4.30 in the morning, we stood on the end of the platform, watching the train crawl through the blue-green mist of the forest, into the clearing, and draw up with the first wounded from Vitry-le-Francois. It was packed with dead and dying and badly wounded. For a time we forgot our weariness in a race against time—removing the dead and dying, and attending to those in need. I was bandaging a man's shattered arm with the *majeur* instructing me, while he stitched a horrible gap in his head, when Madame de A——, the heroic president of the post, came and replaced me. 'There is an English in the fifth wagon,' she said. 'He wants something—I think a holy picture!'

"The idea of an English soldier wanting a holy picture struck me, even in that atmosphere of blood and misery, as something to smile at—but I hurried away. 'The English' was a Lancashire Fusilier. He was propped in a corner, his left arm tied-up in a peasant woman's handkerchief, and his head newly bandaged. He should have been in a state of collapse from loss of blood, for his tattered uniform was soaked and caked in blood, and his face paper-white under the dirt of conflict. He looked at me with bright, courageous eyes and asked for a picture or a medal (he didn't care which) of St. George. I asked him if he was a Catholic. 'No,' he was Wesleyan Methodist, ... and he wanted a picture or a medal of St. George, *because he had seen him on a white horse*, leading the British at Vitry-le-Francois, when the Allies turned.

"There was an F.R.A. man, wounded in the leg, sitting beside him on the floor; he saw my look of amazement, and hastened in: 'It's true, sister,' he said. 'We all saw it. First there was a sort of yellow-mist like, sort of risin' before the Germans as they came on the top of the hill—come on like a solid wall, they did—springing out of the earth just solid—no end to 'em! I just give up. No use fighting the whole German race, thinks I; it's all up with *us*. The next minute comes this funny cloud of light, and when it clears off, there's a tall man with yellow hair in golden armour, on a white horse, holding his sword up, and his mouth open as if he was saying: "Come on, boys! I'll put the kybosh on the devils!" Sort of "This is my picnic" expression. Then, before you could say "knife," the Germans had turned, and we were after them, fighting like ninety....'

"'Where was this?' I asked. But neither of them could tell. They had marched, fighting a rearguard action, from Mons, till St. George had appeared through the haze of light, and turned the enemy. They both *knew* it was St. George. Hadn't they seen him with a sword on every 'quid' they'd ever seen? The Frenchies had seen him too—ask them; but they said it was St. Michæl...."

Much additional testimony of a like nature might be given—and has been collected by students of psychical research. If the spiritual world ever intervenes in matters mundane, it assuredly did so on this occasion. And it could hardly have chosen a more opportune time. Could the aspiring thoughts of the dead and dying, and those still living and fighting for their country, have drawn "St. George" to earth, to aid in again redeeming his country from a foreign foe? Could a simple "hallucination" have been so widespread and so prevalent? Or might there not have been some spiritual energy behind the visions thus seen—stimulating them, and inspiring and encouraging the stricken soldiers? We cannot say. We only know what the soldiers themselves say; and we also know the undoubted effects upon the enemy. For on both occasions were the Germans repulsed with terrible slaughter. Perhaps the vision of St. George led our soldiers into closer touch and *rapport* with the consciousness of some high intelligence—or the veil was rent, separating the two worlds—as so often appears to be the case in apparitions and visions of this character.

APPENDIX C

BIBLIOGRAPHY

Ghost Stories of an Antiquary. M. R. James.
Wandering Ghosts. F. Marion Crawford.
John Silence. A. Blackwood.
Modern Ghosts. DeMaupassant, (and others).
Twenty-five Ghost Stories. W. Bob Holland.
A Book of Ghosts. Baring Gould.
The Shape of Fear. Peattie.
Book of Dreams and Ghosts. Andrew Lang.
Cock Lane and Common Sense. A. Lang.
Real Ghost Stories. W. T. Stead.
More Ghost Stories. W. T. Stead.
The Great Amherst Mystery. Walter Hubbell.
The Bell Witch. M. V. Ingram.
The Alleged Haunting of B—— House. Miss X.
Haunted Houses and Haunted Men. Hon. John Harris.
Ghostly Phenomena. Elliott O'Donnell.
Byways of Ghost Land. Elliott O'Donnell.
Historic Ghosts and Ghost Hunters. H. A. Bruce.
Posthumous Humanity: a Study of Phantoms. D'Assier.

Apparitions and Thought-Transference. Frank Podmore.
The New View of Ghosts. F. Podmore.
Proceedings and *Journals* of the S. P. R.
Borderland (Magazine). Ed. by W. T. Stead.
Haunted Houses of Great Britain. Ingraham.
The Night Side of Nature. Catherine Crowe.
The House and the Brain. Bulwer Lytton.
Nightmare Tales. H. P. Blavatsky.
Apparitions: a Narrative of Facts. B. W. Saville.
Startling Ghost Stories. Anon.
Sights and Shadows. F. G. Lee.
Dracula. Bram Stoker.
The Phantom of the Opera. Gaston Leroux.

[NOTE.—The above list does not pretend to be in any way exhaustive nor are the books quoted in any way equal in evidential value. They are merely types or examples of Ghost Stories, from various points of view; which, if the reader is interested, he may read with both pleasure and profit.]

THE SOCIABLE GHOST

Written down by OLIVE HARPER and ANOTHER

12mo.   235 Pages.   Paper Bound.   With 14 Full-Page Illustrations by Thomas McIlvaine and A. W. Schwartz.

This is a humorous story, giving the adventures of a reporter who was invited by the sociable ghost to a grand banquet, ball, and convention under the ground of Old Trinity Churchyard. A true tale of the things he saw and did not see while he was not there.

Gruesome in spite of its playful humor, as any tale dealing exclusively with skeletons is bound to be, this story in which a New York reporter spends an evening with the illustrious dead in Trinity churchyard, sets the reader to thinking as well as laughing. Instead of burlesquing the departed dead, the author intends to set up a few offenses for which mortals will be punished in the hereafter, and at the same time she protests against the removal of corpses from one cemetery to another to afford space for the tramp of onward civilization.

The sociable ghost, who was formerly a society leader in the metropolis, takes the curious reporter into the banqueting hall of the dead elite, where ghosts, not sufficiently purified in soul to go free from the hindrance of bones and burdened with their mundane characteristics, dance, gormandize, simper and gossip as they did during life, waiting for the passports the Master promises to give when the taint of earthly vices and frivolities have been purged. Particularly amusing is the passage in which some sinner is compelled to teach five ladies of the "400" how to play poker, as well as the place where the guests are compelled to repeat for the edification and amusement of each other the terrible epitaphs that disfigure their tombstones.

This book is for sale by all dealers everywhere, or it will be sent by mail, postpaid, on receipt of **price, 50 cents**. Address all orders to

J. S. OGILVIE PUBLISHING COMPANY
57 ROSE STREET, NEW YORK

OGILVIE'S
ASTROLOGICAL BIRTHDAY BOOK

Your birthday is the most important day in your life. And yet how few people realize the importance and significance of that event! Out of all eternity, how came it about that you were born just when you were? Wise men who have thought on this question say that this cannot be due to mere chance; there must be some reason, some law, at work. They set about ascertaining this law—which relates to the time of birth—and discovered it in the science of *Astrology*.

Every one is born under slightly different influence and circumstances; so no two people are exactly alike. This, says Astrology, is because the aspects of the heavens—the influences brought to bear upon the infant at the moment of birth—are so different.

To test the claims of astrology, it is only necessary to have a personal reading made of the life. For this, the exact date and hour of birth is necessary—so that the various combinations and aspects of the planets may be figured out accurately; but, while this individual reading is, of course, by far the most satisfactory—nevertheless, certain signs and aspects are said to influence all born on a certain day, in some degree.

Oglivie's Astrological Birthday Book contains a character reading for every day in the year based on observations of the aspects of the heavenly bodies on the day of birth.

It is useful as a guide to the course in life which you should pursue to achieve the greatest degree of success by the use of your known talents, and by the development of your latent or potential abilities in the field of endeavor to which you are naturally adapted. More than being useful, it is a source of much entertainment at a gathering to read aloud the characters of those present.

The book contains 264 pages printed on antique wove book paper, attractively bound in cloth, with jacket printed in colors. Price, **75 cents** by mail, postpaid.

J. S. OGILVIE PUBLISHING COMPANY

P. O. Box 767. 57 ROSE STREET, NEW YORK

OGILVIE'S POPULAR COPYRIGHT LINE

THE FORTUNES OF BETTY. By Cecil Spooner. Love, romance, pathos, sympathy, martial spirit, reverence, action—all have their place and a share in the success-making and attention-holding qualities of Miss Spooner's novel. It is a story of a small-town girl, who strives to keep the honor of the family name intact, and who by her ability, ready wit, and bravery, succeeds in overcoming the machinations of rich and powerful enemies. The admiration and reverence due the Stars and Stripes, and those who fought under them, is graphically depicted; and Betty's difficulties in winning the love of the man upon whom her affections are bestowed are admirably set forth. It is pure in thought, tender in motive, and true to the higher ideals of life and love. **Price, 60 cents, postpaid.**

THE CONFESSIONS OF A PRINCESS. The writer has taken a page from her life and has given it to the world. She has laid bare the soul of a woman, that some other woman (or some man) might profit thereby. Her disposition and character were such as to compel her to find elsewhere than in her own home the love, tenderness, admiration, and society which was lacking there, and which her being craved. The names have been changed and such events omitted as might lead too readily to the discovery of identities. Each the victim of a circumstance over  which they had no control, yet the *price* is demanded of the one who fell the victim of environment. *The Confessions of a Princess* is the story of a woman who saw, conquered and fell.

'WAY DOWN EAST. By Joseph R. Grismer. One of the sweetest stories of New England life ever written; one full of the love and tenderness made possible by honest Christian living among pure, whole-hearted, and broad-minded country folks. This book is founded upon the play, which, with ever-increasing popularity, has been presented so often to the American public. Over 300,000 copies of the book have been sold. Have you read it? If not, why not get it now? **Price. 60 cents, postpaid.**

ONE HUNDRED DOG STORIES; or, Dogs of All Nations. This collection of stories grew naturally out of a child's demand for more, and still more, stories about dogs. They teach a strong moral lesson of love, honesty and fidelity. 76 illustrations.

The above books are library size, printed on excellent paper, handsomely and substantially bound in cloth. **Price, postpaid, 75 cents each, unless otherwise stated.**

J. S. OGILVIE PUBLISHING COMPANY
57 Rose Street, New York

OGILVIE'S POPULAR COPYRIGHT LINE

THE MYSTERY OF THE RAVENSPURS. By Fred M. White A romantic tale of adventure, mystery and amateur detective work, with scenes laid in England, India, and the distant and comparatively unknown Thibet. A band of mystics from the latter country are the prime movers in the various conspiracies, and their new, unique, weird, strange methods form one of the features of the story.

THE FORGED COUPON. By Count Leo Tolstoi. This story shows the successive evil and wrong resulting from the forging of a note by a student in need of money. Numerous crimes succeed each other as a result of this first wrong act, until the wave of crime is checked by a poor, ignorant woman and a lame tailor, who follow the real teaching of Christ. The book contains also *After the Ball*, a story of love and military life; *Korney Vasilyev*, a story of peasant life; *Tolstoi's Vital Humanitarian Ideas*, giving the very essence of the fountain-spring and incentive of all the literary work ever written by this wonderful man—a peep, as it were, at the power-works of his thinking machine.

THE KREUTZER SONATA. By Count Leo Tolstoi. A book which has a world-wide reputation, in fact, the one that made its author famous, and one which everyone of mature years should read. The closing words of the book show the nature of the moral to be deduced: "Yes, that is what I have done, that is my experience. We must understand the real meaning of the words of the Gospel—Matthew V, 28—which relate to the wife, to the sister, and not only to the wife of another, but especially to one's own wife." The moral lesson to be learned is plainly visible, and its solution is the solution of the "higher mind."

ANNA KARENINE. By Count Leo Tolstoi. Another story by this famous Russian, depicting the trials and temptations that beset a young woman, showing the development of character under trying ordeals and circumstances. Second only to the author's *Kreutzer Sonata*, for his perfect understanding of the impulses that govern the relations of the sexes.

The above books are library size, printed on excellent paper, handsomely and substantially bound in cloth.
Price, postpaid, 75 cents each, unless otherwise stated.

J. S. OGILVIE PUBLISHING COMPANY
57 Rose Street, New York

OGILVIE'S POPULAR COPYRIGHT LINE

"FOMA GORDEYEV." By Maxime Gorky. This book made Gorky's literary reputation in Russia, Germany and France. It is a most remarkable novel. The *New York Evening Post* says:

"Maxime Gorky, the young Russian poet of the vagabond and the proletariat, the most ardent worshipper at the shrine of Nietzsche and his ideal 'Over-Man,' owes much of his sudden popularity to his personality. The son of a poor upholsterer, Gorky was thrown upon his own resources at the age of nine and since then has experienced a wide range of human emotions, struggles, depravity and misery. Shoemaker, apple peddler, painter, dock-hand, railroad workman, baker and tramp, this unique author had a thousand and one similar occupations, and had even made more than one attempt to take his own life."

This version of *Foma Gordeyev*, is in no way abridged, giving the exact reproduction of the thought and expression of the author.

THE SEVEN WHO WERE HANGED. By Leonid Andreyev. What reviewers say:

"Andreyev is greater than Poe—greater for his truth if not for his art."—*St. Louis Mirror*.

"It is by reason of its art even more real, more horrifying, more impressive than any other Russian fiction translated in a long time. Under the crystal simplicity of Andreyev's style each spirit reveals itself, stripped of its bodily covering, in its inmost truth."—*New York Times*.

"Grewsome, because it is fearfully real. But it is compelling for the same reason."—*New York World*.

"You rise from the book with a shudder—which is a tribute to its power—and with the firm conviction that capital punishment is a crime—another tribute to its author's genius."—*Kentucky Post*.

"It is not a mere morbid probing into the abormal and horrible. It has its mission. It is a grim and terrible picture, and it is painted with tremendous art—the art of a Dore."—*Chicago Inter-Ocean*.
Price, 60 cents, postpaid.

THE SHORT CUT. By G. Elliott Flint. A novel of tense, palpitating, throbbing, passionate life and love, with scenes laid around New York's "Great White Way," setting forth the conflicting tendencies of good and evil, worldly desire and control of self. The magnetism of sex is the pivot on which the world revolves. The truth is inevitable. Why close our eyes to facts?

The above books are library size, printed on excellent paper, handsomely and substantially bound in cloth.
Price, postpaid, 75 cents each, unless otherwise stated.

J. S. OGILVIE PUBLISHING COMPANY
57 Rose Street, New York

OGILVIE'S POPULAR COPYRIGHT LINE

THE EMPEROR'S CANDLESTICKS. By Baroness Orczy. A story of Nihilism and Russian Court intrigue, in which a powerful band of Nihilists with strong Court connections have their most cherished plans frustrated through the miscarriage of one of their messages concealed in one of the candlesticks, the other candlestick bearing a message concerning a secret love affair of the Russian Emperor. The complications which ensue keep the reader at a tense pitch of excitement, which is only assuaged when the story ends; how, of course it would not be fair to say. The Baroness Orczy is sufficiently well known as an author, however, to guarantee a pleasurable and profitable book.

THE SILENT BATTLE. By Mrs. C. N. Williamson. The battle in question is between a powerful, well-known multi-millionaire of London, and a beautiful, talented, charming young actress who rejects the approaches and attentions of the former. She is ably assisted in her fight for existence by a strong, handsome American, who is in London on a secret quest. Their paths meet, and they eventually work together against the common enemy. Honor, love, position, and a fortune are the prizes of battle, and its fighting, is told in the interesting way for which Mrs. C. N. Williamson is justly famous.

THE TESTING OF OLIVE VAUGHAN. By Percy J. Brebner. A story of the stage showing the temptations to which every aspirant for theatrical fame and fortune is subject, and showing too, how, through right decisions and correct judgment based on inborn and developing strength of character one is able to rise superior to her surroundings and wrest a great success. This is not easy to accomplish, however, and its telling, which shows a fine literary style and unquestioned powers of characterization and description, is what makes the author one of the most popular among fiction writers of the present day.

The above books are library size, printed on excellent paper, handsomely and substantially bound in cloth. Price, postpaid, 75 cents each, unless otherwise stated.

J. S. OGILVIE PUBLISHING COMPANY
57 Rose Street, New York

OGILVIE'S POPULAR COPYRIGHT LINE

THE PEER AND THE WOMAN. By E. Phillips Oppenheim. A story of romance, mystery, and adventure, in which a peer of England, notwithstanding his breeding and social position, becomes entangled with a scheming adventuress, until he is mysteriously put out of the way. From this point on complication and adventure succeed each other in rapid succession, holding the reader in rapt fascination to the end, where the plots of love and mysterious disappearances are surprisingly unfolded.

A MONK OF CRUTA. By E. Phillips Oppenheim. One of the stories that made the author famous. It is full of mystery, love and adventure, and from the first chapter, which is laid in a familiar and well-known monastery, to the last, the reader follows the characters with increasing interest. It is the kind of a book to take away over the holidays, or read in the evenings at home, as it has that "grip" which makes it a relaxation to read. It banishes care and trouble, and lifts you out of yourself by its strongly woven plot.

THE NEW MAYOR. Founded upon George Broadhurst's Play *The Man of the Hour*. A strong story of politics, love and graft, which appeals powerfully to every true American. The play has reeived the highest praise and commendation from critics and the press.

"The finest play I ever saw."
—THEODORE ROOSEVELT.

"The best in years."—*N. Y. Telegram*.
"A triumph."—*N. Y. American*.
"A sensation."—*N. Y. Herald*.
"Means something."—*N. Y. Tribune*.
"Best play yet."—*N. Y. Commercial*.
"A play worth while."—*N. Y. News*.
"A straight hit."—*N. Y. World*. "An apt appeal."—*N. Y. Globe*.
"A perfect success."—*N. Y. Sun*. "An object lesson."—*N. Y. Post*.
Price, 60 cents, postpaid.

WHITE DANDY, The Story of a Horse. By V. C. Melville. Everyone interested in horses should read this charming story. It stands shoulder to shoulder with the famous book *Black Beauty* for pathos, heart interest and gentleness. If the two books above mentioned were read with all the attention which they should command, we would have less cause to complain of the cruelty to animals from brutal masters. Price, 50 cents, postpaid.

The above books are library size, printed on excellent paper, handsomely and substantially bound in cloth.
Price, postpaid, 75 cents each, unless otherwise stated.

J. S. OGILVIE PUBLISHING COMPANY
57 Rose Street, New York

OGILVIE'S POPULAR COPYRIGHT LINE

THE DEVIL. By Ferenc Molnar. A strong, moral book, showing in a vivid, realistic manner the result of evil thinking. *The Devil* in this story is evil thinking materialized. It deals with the early love of a poor artist and a poor maiden. As the years go by the artist achieves distinction, and the maiden becomes the wife of a millionaire merchant — with very little romance in his composition, but thoroughly devoted to his young and beautiful bride. Seven years later the artist (who has been received as a valued friend of the family) is commissioned to paint the wife's portrait—and the old love reasserts itself. For a while the issue is problematical; but stability of character conquers, and the ending is quite as the heart would wish. **Price, 60 cents, postpaid.**

THE "MAN IN THE STREET STORIES." From *The New York Times*, with an introduction by Chauncey M. Depew, who says of them: "This collection of stories is my refresher every Sunday after the worry and work of the week. I know of no effort which has been so successful in collecting real anecdotes and portraying the humorous side of life as this volume." It is prepared with a complete index, which increases its value very much. Read what reviewers all over the country say of the book:

"It is a great collection, and the reading of it is a treat."—*Salt Lake Tribune*.

"The kind of a book we call a 'capital thing.' Its humor is of the best flavor."—*Minneapolis Times*.

"Warranted to amuse."—*Boston Journal*.

"Probably no book of its kind excells this one."—*Detroit Free Press*.

"The anecdotes are exceptionally entertaining, full of humor, wit and wisdom, and may be read with genuine pleasure."—*St. Louis Republic*.

"Full of good things."—*Philadelphia Inquirer*.

NATHAN HALE, The Martyr Spy. By Chas. W. Brown. This is a story of the American Revolution, founded upon the play of the same name, upon a subject which will never grow old as this brave man's name will go down in history as a hero, as a martyr, whose famous saying, "My only regret is that I have but one poor life to give to my country," is world-wide known. **Price, 50 cents, postpaid.**

The above books are library size, printed on excellent paper, handsomely and substantially bound in cloth. **Price, postpaid, 75 cents each, unless otherwise stated.**

J. S. OGILVIE PUBLISHING COMPANY
57 Rose Street, New York

OGILVIE'S POPULAR COPYRIGHT LINE

ARSENE LUPIN, Gentleman Burglar, and ARSENE LUPIN *versus* HERLOCK SHOLMES. By Maurice Leblanc. Maurice Leblanc can be compared only to A. Conan Doyle. With Sherlock Holmes one is each time facing a new robbery and a new crime. With *Arsene Lupin* we know in advance he is the guilty one. We know, that when we shall have unravelled the tangled threads of the story, we shall find ourselves facing the famous *Gentleman Burglar*. But with the aid of processes which the most adept are not able to fathom, the author holds your attention to the very end of each adventure, and the dramatic termination is always the unexpected. *Arsene Lupin* does not steal, he simply amuses himself by stealing. He chooses, at need he restores. He is noble, charming, chivalrous, delicate. Thief and burglar, robber and confidence man, anything you could wish, but so sympathetic—the bandit! If you appreciate skill, ability, resourcefulness, and a battle between master-minds, do not fail to read these two books.

A GENTLEMAN FROM MISSISSIPPI. A novel founded upon the play of the same name. Senator Langdon is picked out by dishonest men in Washington to be used as their tool in the Senate. But the "tool" proves to be sharp at both ends and cuts the men who mean to cheat the people. Honesty attracts honesty, and Langdon draws to his side as his secretary "Bud" Haines, one who is as shrewd as the dishonest senators, and together they prove more than a match for all the rascality in Washington. Just how Langdon accomplishes his ends is one of the most interesting parts of the book —and even Langdon himself doesn't know how he is going to win out until the last moment—then he wins by simple honesty. **Price, 60 cents, postpaid.**

The above books are library size, printed on excellent paper, handsomely and substantially bound in cloth.
Price, postpaid, 75 cents each, unless otherwise stated.

J. S. OGILVIE PUBLISHING COMPANY
57 Rose Street, New York

OGILVIE'S POPULAR COPYRIGHT LINE

RESURRECTION. By Count Leo Tolstoi. It depicts with a master hand the ocean of life rocked by storm and lulled to sleep and ease. In the splash of every wave is heard the story of human emotions, misery, disenchantment, suffering, crime, and life, that is true—even in art. Nekhludov, the central figure, is a powerful, unfathomable stroke of artistic genius. He is not always a hero—he is a man—hence heir to weakness and temptation. Passion runs wild in him. The beast, the flesh, triumph over the spirit. In wine, women, and corruption he forgets the victim of his crime, and were it not for an almost improbable coincidence, his soul, his conscience, would never awaken. But he becomes a new man; and it is the telling of this which gives *Resurrection* its power.

THE HOUSE BY THE RIVER. By Florence Warden. A wonderful story of mystery and romance, one in which, to the reader's mind, every character in the book is guilty until the end is reached. Read what the reviewers say of it:

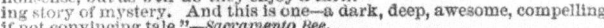

"Florence Warden is the Anna Katharine Green of England. She apparently has the same marvelous capacity as Mrs. Rohlfs for concocting the most complicated plots and most mystifying mysteries."—*N. Y. Globe.*

"The interest of the story is deep and intense."—*Salt Lake Tribune.*

"The author has a knack of intricate plot-work which will keep an intelligent reader at *her* books, when he would become tired over far better novels. For even the wisest men' now and then relish not only a little nonsense, but as well do they enjoy a thrilling story of mystery. And this is one—a dark, deep, awesome, compelling if not convincing tale."—*Sacramento Bee.*

THE WORLD'S FINGER. By T. W. Hanshew. It is a scientific theory that the retina of the eye of a dying person will retain the impression, or photograph, as you might call it, of any object that it rests upon if seen at the instant of death. *The World's Finger* is a detective story in which this theory plays a prominent part. A lawyer wrote us stating that he never before read a book in which the chain of convicting evidence was so complete, but in which the suspected criminal was finally found innocent.

The above books are library size, printed on excellent paper, handsomely and substantially bound in cloth.
Price, postpaid, 75 cents each, unless otherwise stated.

J. S. OGILVIE PUBLISHING COMPANY
57 Rose Street, New York

OTHER BOOKS ABOUT THE SUPERNATURAL FROM CURIOUS PUBLICATIONS

The History of Spiritualism (Vols. 1 & 2)
by Sir Arthur Conan Doyle

The Case for Spirit Photography
by Sir Arthur Conan Doyle

Psycho-Phone Messages
by Francis Grierson

*Spectropia, or Surprising Spectral Illusions
Showing Ghosts Everywhere*
by J. H. Brown

Spirit Slate Writing and Kindred Phenomena
by William E. Robinson

How to Speak With the Dead: A Practical Handbook
by Sciens

*The Talking Dead: A Collection of Messages from
Beyond the Veil, 1850s-1920s*
Edited by Marc Hartzman

Vampires and Vampirism
by Dudley Wright

The Book of Dreams and Ghosts
by Andrew Lang

curiouspublications.com

www.ingramcontent.com/pod-product-compliance
Lightning Source LLC
Chambersburg PA
CBHW030014040426
42337CB00012BA/782